‖‖‖ ‖ ‖‖‖‖‖‖‖ ‖ ‖ ‖ ‖‖‖‖‖‖‖‖‖‖ ‖‖ ‖‖ ‖‖‖
W9-AKC-458

More praise for
The Pocket Guide to Prayer

"Filled with practical suggestions and gentle encouragement for those who are beginning to pray as well as those who wish to reexamine their prayer lives. Well grounded in theology and psychology, Egeberg's writing presents the possibility of a deep experience of prayer. I particularly appreciate the prayers at the end of each chapter that summarize the content and guide the reader to the heart of the teachings."

> —Rev. Jane E. Vennard, Iliff School of Theology, author of *Praying with Body and Soul*

"Gary Egeberg is a comfortable and reassuring companion for our journey toward God. He promises to enhance our understanding of God and prayer and to enrich our prayer life—and he delivers. This book is realistic, practical, and completely non-threatening."

> —Carol Luebering, author of *A Retreat with Job and Julian of Norwich*

"Viewing our hunger for a relationship with the Divine against today's hectic life-style, Egeberg alerts us to the prayer already existing in our lives and encourages us to expand our dimensions of prayer. Having been drawn into this book, we are drawn into prayer itself."

> —Theresa Cotter, author of *Called to Preside: A Handbook for Laypeople*

"A treasury of modest wisdom and balanced spirituality, a power pack."
—William Cleary, author of How the Wild Things Pray

"A beautiful, inspiring, and encouraging book for ordinary people who want a closer relationship with God. Gary Egeberg's simple and direct approach speaks to the heart. This guide to prayer contains a rich array of suggestions to jump start your prayer life. If you are stressed out and need a spirit-energizer, The Pocket Guide to Prayer will soothe your soul and provide food for your hungry heart. I highly recommend this book."
—Dr. Bridget Mary Meehan, author of Praying with Women of the Bible

"Gary Egeberg offers practical suggestions and lively examples in a simple, direct way. Clearly, he teaches from his own experiences as both apprentice and journeyman on the path of prayer."
—Virginia Ann Froehle, R.S.M., spiritual director and author of Loving Yourself More: 101 Meditations for Women

"Packed with useful information and authentic inspiration. An excellent companion for newcomers to prayer, and a necessary reminder of what is important for those of us who still haven't got it right after all these years—and that's probably most of us. It is helpful, gentle, and wise."
—Michael Leach, Executive Director, Orbis Books

The Pocket Guide to Prayer

"For those who seek spiritual depth, this book is perfect. It provides specific guidance in developing a devotional life that creates inner fulfillment and service towards others."

   —Tony Campolo, Eastern College, St. Davids, Pennsylvania

The Pocket Guide
to Prayer

Gary Egeberg

MINNEAPOLIS

THE POCKET GUIDE TO PRAYER

Copyright © 1999 Augsburg Fortress. All rights reserved. Except for brief quotations in critical articles or reviews, no part of this book may be reproduced in any manner without prior written permission from the publisher. Write to: Permissions, Augsburg Fortress, Box 1209, Minneapolis, MN 55440.

Cover design by Craig Claeys
Book design by Michelle L. Norstad
Spiral cover art from PhotoDisc, Inc.
Phone booth cover art from Randy Wells/Tony Stone Images.

Acknowledgments
Scripture passages, unless otherwise marked, are from the New Revised Standard Version © 1989 by the Division of Christian Education of the National Council of the Churches of Christ in the United States of America. Used by permission.

Scripture texts marked NAB are taken from the New American Bible, copyright © 1970 by the Confraternity of Christian Doctrine, Washington, D.C., and are used by permission of the copyright owner. All rights reserved.

Library of Congress Cataloging-in-Publication Data
Egeberg, Gary, 1953–
  The pocket guide to prayer / Gary Egeberg.
    p. cm.
  Includes bibliographical references.
  ISBN 0-8066-3958-X (alk. paper)
  1. Prayer—Christianity. I. Title.
BV210.2.E335 1999
248.3'2—dc21   99-34648
                                                            CIP

The paper used in this publication meets the minimum requirements of American National Standard for Information Sciences—Permanence of Paper for Printed Library Materials, ANSI Z329.48-1984. ⊖ ™

Manufactured in the U.S.A.   AF 9-3958

                        4   5   6   7   8   9   10

DEDICATION

FOR MY FATHER, RUBEN N. EGEBERG, whose faith was and is a guiding force in his life. Like many fathers and sons, we had our struggles early on, but I am more convinced than ever before that love is the strongest force in the universe and has the last—and lasting—word.

Thank you for your love and support and for always being willing to help me along my life's journey.

CONTENTS

Acknowledgments 11

Introduction 13

Chapter 1   God, Prayer, and Our Expectations . . 17

Chapter 2   Getting Started 34

Chapter 3   Listening for God's Voice 49

Chapter 4   Answers to Prayer 62

Chapter 5   Praying with the Bible 79

Chapter 6   Resting in God 96

Chapter 7   Praying Our Pain and Suffering . . 113

Chapter 8   A Well-Balanced Prayer Life 130

Suggestions for Further Reading 145

Acknowledgments

Deepest gratitude to my wife, Peggy, whose loving presence in my life means so very much to me as a writer, teacher, parent, and husband.

Thank you to my daughters, Kristen and Erica, who have helped me rediscover wonder-vision and whose unconditional love for me is among the greatest of all gifts.

Special thanks to my spiritual director, John Koller, for sharing your knowledge, wisdom, and companionate presence with me. You have helped me find my way many times in years past, and I look forward to journeying with you in the years to come.

I extend my appreciation to my editor at Augsburg Books, Martha Rosenquist, for your friendliness, laughter, and wonderful editorial suggestions.

Thank you to Michelle Norstad, my production editor, who so graciously allowed me to make a number of last-minute changes.

Finally, thank you to the many authors whose insights on prayer and spirituality have been so helpful to me over the years. I am sure that much of what I share in this book is a result of the seeds you unknowingly planted in my life.

INTRODUCTION

THOMAS MERTON, THE TRAPPIST monk and prolific twentieth-century writer on prayer and spirituality, once wrote, "If you have never had any distractions you don't know how to pray." That's terrific news for those of us who may have felt inept in our attempts to pray *because* of our persistent distractions and *because* of the unending stream of thoughts that tend to arise when we turn our hearts and minds to God in prayer! Merton, along with a host of other prayer teachers, also suggests that prayer is a hunger for God, a hunger that goes deeper than our ability—or inability—to keep our thoughts focused on God.

Many of us are aware of our hunger for God and long to have a better prayer life. Yet too often, both God and prayer seem to remain just out of reach. We want to pray, but we are pulled in so many other directions at home, work, and elsewhere. We struggle to devote enough time and energy to our families and friends, and have discovered that taking the time to care for ourselves—including some time for prayer—is an ongoing challenge.

When we do take some time to sit down and pray, our thoughts frequently do not sit down with us. In fact, they start to fly away from here to there, with little hope of calling them back. Or, if it's not our own inner discord that pulls us away from prayer, the outer discord does: the phone rings, the kids start to fight, a deadline at work beckons us, or some other situation demanding our attention arises. For some of us, we reach the point where it becomes easier not to pray, not because we don't believe in the value of prayer or in God's love for us, but because it is just too hard to do, too elusive, in the reality of our daily lives. In short, we become discouraged. Prayer is not satisfying, so the hunger for God and prayer remains unfulfilled. Yet we continue to hunger.

This book is about discovering some simple and practical ways to pray so that we might better satisfy our hunger for God. We will also try to gain a better understanding of prayer by probing a few of its mysteries. For instance, we will try to gain some insights into how God communicates with us and how God answers our prayers.

We will begin our journey together by taking a quick glance at what we may have been taught about God and prayer during our childhood and decide if we are carrying around any unnecessary baggage that is hindering our prayer life today. We will examine our images of God and learn some ways to expand upon them, which may help to expand and enhance our prayer life as well. We will also assess our expectations of God and prayer and try to let go of those that are unrealistic and cling to those that are more true to our experience.

In this book you will learn how to restart your prayer life, how to set realistic prayer goals, and how to slow down and quiet your restless mind. Specific parts of the Bible that are especially prayer-friendly are identified, as are some concrete suggestions for praying with God's word. You will also discover some practical and refreshing ways to rest in and with God when you are feeling over-whelmed, worried, depressed, or worn out.

No book on prayer is complete without at least attempting to address the mystery of pain and suffering, so we will consider some guidelines that may help us cope with our suffering and identify some ways to turn toward God with our pain, including the pain we feel for others. Finally, we will explore some of the components of a well-balanced prayer life and touch on, among other things, the importance of expressing gratitude, interceding on behalf of others, and seeking forgiveness, so that we might come to know experientially the positive, powerful, and healing impact prayer has in life.

Once again, the primary aim of this book is to offer some specific and practical ideas to help make prayer more meaningful and to better satisfy the God-given hunger God has placed within our hearts for divine love. With that in mind, it is my hope that this pocket guide to prayer will be helpful to you as you spend time with the one whose passionate love for you is endless and unconditional.

CHAPTER 1

GOD, PRAYER, AND OUR EXPECTATIONS

 The best reason to pray is that God is really there.

—Emilie Griffin

SOMEWHERE DEEP INSIDE, OUR hearts yearn for the God who loves and accepts us unconditionally. We crave closeness with God and long for God's strength, compassion, and forgiveness. We want to know that God really is there for each of us as individuals and for all of humanity.

Prayer is one powerful way to experience the presence of God in our daily lives, however, most of us have discovered that much can get in the way of spending time with God. One barrier is the rather strict limitations we have placed upon prayer. Some of us have unintentionally defined prayer too narrowly or have confined ourselves to praying in just one particular way. For instance, maybe you were taught, as I was, to sit down, close your eyes, fold your hands, and then talk to God. This is a good way to pray, but other good ways of praying are waiting to be discovered. One of these just might help us break free when we get stuck, focus a little better when we are restless and distracted, or experience a little more satisfaction when prayer has become an empty struggle.

Before we consider a variety of ways to pray, it can be helpful to expand our definition of prayer, examine our understandings and images of the one to whom we are directing our prayers, and clearly identify our expectations—which may or may not be realistic—of God and prayer.

Because I had defined prayer too narrowly and had restricted myself to praying in only one way for much of my life, I never even knew there were other ways to pray. For example, I didn't know it was possible to write some of my prayers until someone suggested I give it a try. It has proven to be a good way for me to pray, especially when I am troubled or have a lot on my mind. As my understanding of prayer continued to expand, I became willing to experiment with other "new" ways of praying. I embraced some and discarded others as I learned to trust my ability to discern what did and did not work for me.

During all of my childhood and many of my adult years, I had only one image and understanding of God, and that was of God as Father. This has been the dominant image of God in Christianity since its beginning. Many people find it to be a wonderful image of God, while others are less attracted to it. For some, the father image is even a barrier to drawing closer to God. For me, it has become a better image for God than it once was because it is no longer my only image of God. Just as I need more than one way to pray, I need more than one image of God. In this chapter, we will look at how we acquired our images of God during our formative years and learn some simple ways to add to our images of God today, but first a word about expectations.

Our expectations of virtually anything and anyone set us up to experience disappointment, delight, or something in between. We all have expectations of God and prayer, many of which began in childhood and some of which haven't been consciously examined or altered since.

In my own life, I used to think—and sometimes still think—that my role in prayer is to tell God what needs to be done and how to do it. And then when God doesn't follow my suggestions, orders, or commands, I experience frustration and disappointment. It's all because I have the unexamined expectation that prayer is telling or reminding God of what needs to be done and how to do it. Slowly and more than a bit reluctantly, I do it less than I once did, but I suspect I will probably offer God some free advice on how to run the world at various times during the rest of my life.

Later in this chapter, we will uncover some of the unrealistic expectations we may have of God and prayer and identify some realistic ones to keep in mind with the hopes of experiencing more satisfaction, rather than disappointment, and perhaps an occasional dose of delight in our dance with God.

What Is Prayer? How Should We Pray?

One of the "problems" of prayer is that it is so broad, diverse, and all-encompassing that it can seem ungraspable. Because so much has been said and written about prayer throughout the ages, and because every religion and spiritual path offers a variety of interpretations about the nature of God and the practice of prayer, we can easily feel overwhelmed. It can be like trying to choose a meal from a restaurant offering a thousand entrees! At the same time, one of the "solutions" to prayer is its broadness and diversity, because it allows each and every person of varying religions and no religion to find his or her niche in the heart of God.

One of the goals of this book is to break down the inexact and vast art of prayer into something that is more manageable and enriching so that we can become increasingly aware of how near God is and how eager God is to help us in life. We can work with God to simplify the enormity of the menu and, hopefully, discover a few satisfying and nourishing prayer entrees along the way. Let's begin by looking at a few definitions or descriptions of prayer:

- Prayer is being aware of God's presence in our lives and in our world.
- Prayer is our attempts to turn our hearts, minds, and entire selves toward God.
- Prayer is spending time with God in friendship and partnership.
- Prayer is experiencing wonder and amazement at the beauty in the world.

- Prayer is a desire to draw close to God.
- Prayer is talking, listening, and being with God in silent and mutual love.
- Prayer is turning to God with our needs and wants and placing our trust in God.
- Prayer is opening up and tapping in to God's love and power.
- Prayer is a relationship requiring active participation from both God and us.
- Prayer is rediscovering God's loving and intimate involvement in our lives.

Pause, Ponder, or Practice

Which of the previous prayer descriptions best fit your current understanding or definition of prayer? Which of them expand your understanding of prayer? What thoughts about prayer would you add to this list?

Perhaps your own definition of prayer or one of the ten thoughts above has helped to clarify, simplify, or expand what prayer means for you. Now, let's direct our attention to three characteristics of prayer we might strive to develop.

Pray from the heart. This means we pray sincerely, openly, and honestly. We try not to hide things from God and we don't pray halfheartedly. The way to pray from the heart is to share your experiences with God. Share with God the thoughts and feelings you are experiencing at this moment. Feelings of anger, grief, restlessness, boredom, hate, jealousy, and resentment are as acceptable to bring to God in prayer as are feelings of joy, peace, gratitude, and hope. If you are questioning God's existence, express it to the God you are not convinced exists. If you are angry with God or someone else—or both—let God know in no uncertain terms how angry you feel!

Pray with your entire self. Prayer is not just what takes place between our ears. It is not just our minds, but also our hearts, our personalities, our bodies, our emotions, our entire selves. We can pray with a variety of traditional and nontraditional postures: kneeling, standing, lying down, folded hands, open hands, and clenched fists, to name but a few. We can pray while walking, sipping a cup of coffee, or commuting to work. We are whole beings, no matter how fragmented we may feel at any given time, so we needn't compartmentalize or separate prayer from our daily experiences.

Pray with trust. It is so important to trust that God is with you at this—and every—moment and is intimately involved in our lives and throughout our world. We might find it difficult to trust God for a variety of reasons—and we certainly can't force trust—but we *can* strive to develop this prayer quality. As we seek out trust, it will become a more trustworthy friend and companion in life.

How We Have Come to Understand and Image God

If we are going to try to pray with trust, with our entire selves, and from the depths of our hearts, we need to open up to the ongoing process of getting to know who God is and what God is like—at least to some degree. For many of us, it all began in childhood. As young children, we may have been introduced to God through our parents, other relatives, and perhaps through our religion or Sunday school teachers. Some of us may have been taught that God loves us, cares for us, and forgives us. Others of us may have picked up the message that God is more interested in judging and punishing us than in helping and befriending us.

Because God was most often, or even exclusively, addressed as "father" and because people frequently used the masculine pronouns "he" and "him" when speaking to or about God, we might have developed an almost indelible image of God as male, often an old man with white hair and a beard. Even today many young children have this image of God. I was surprised when one of my daughters, who was four years old at the time, already had this image of God.

We also came to image God as being like our parents. How our parents loved and cared for us is how we thought God loved and cared for us. If we experienced inconsistent or conditional love or if we were parented in a dysfunctional manner, that is probably how we came to image and understand God. If our early experiences of what we were taught or how we were treated were not the best, we can begin or continue the work of getting to know the true God who is consistently caring and unconditionally loving.

To sum up, we incorporated our images and understandings of God quite early in life and, as is the case with most of our early experiences, it has had a lasting impact. We can choose to keep the early images, understandings, and teachings that were helpful and healing and discard those that were not.

Pause, Ponder, or Practice

What are your earliest memories of what you were taught about God, both who God is and what God is like? Of the adults in your life, who did you see as being most like God? Name both your positive and negative experiences and try to discern which ones are still operating in your life today.

Expanding Our Images of God

✓ God is unknowable, transcendent, and totally beyond us. Therefore, we need to accept the fact that we will never know all there is to know about God, just as there will always be something new to learn about the people we know best. Yet at the same time, ✓ God is knowable, immanent, and very much with us. God is self-revealing and desirous of relationship, so it is possible to get to know God better, just as we can get to know each other better.

When it comes to knowing God, we can increase our knowledge and strengthen our friendship by adding to the images and understandings we have acquired thus far. Here are four suggestions to help us in this process.

1. Make a list of relationships, jobs, and roles people have. Determine which ones help describe God more fully, and focus on the ones you find most appealing. Relationships such as mother, father, sister, brother, grandmother, friend, and partner might be a good place to start. You might consider different jobs and roles such as pastor, doctor, nurse, guide, pilot, and lawyer. Think of the qualities, characteristics, and personal meaning some of these have for you. Perhaps you have had a wonderful relationship with your grandmother or with a caring teacher. See God as having the same qualities as these special people in your life. Or perhaps you can begin to image God defending you against inner or outer critical voices, much like an attorney would defend you in court. If you are sinking under shame or guilt for past failings, maybe thinking of God as having the power a governor or president has to pardon a person on death row might help set you free from your painful past. Images such as these help make our invisible God more concrete and tangible, which we human beings need.

2. Make a list of nouns, adjectives, and descriptive phrases that tell what God is like. Pay special attention to the ones that speak to you. You could do this in a systematic way by starting with the letter *A* and working your way through the alphabet, perhaps with a dictionary in hand: active . . . benevolent . . . concerned. Or you might write down different descriptive words as they come to mind. Another possibility is to take an adjective and turn it in to a noun and address God by a new name, such as Compassion or Mercy or Friend.

Consider recording some names, descriptors, and images for God in a notebook or journal. You might turn to it when you feel a need, or continue adding new images as you discover them.

3. Search a few of the psalms and record the images, descriptors, and actions of God that appeal to you. Try some of these in your prayer. Among the many images and descriptors in the psalms, God is referred to as light, salvation, defender, rock, refuge, fortress, shelter, strength, and shepherd. God's actions include rescuing, saving, teaching, instructing, advising, listening, and coming to our assistance. You might choose to compile one list of names and adjectives and one list of verbs telling what God does for us. Perhaps an image of God as "shelter" will help you feel protected as you experience a conflict with someone, or the image of "rock" might help you better grasp God's secure presence during a shaky time in your life. If you are not familiar with the book of Psalms, you might begin by skimming through Psalms 18, 27, and 71.

4. Look for passages in the Bible which portray God as having feminine and motherly characteristics. Not too many decades ago the roles of each sex were clearly defined: men were supposed to go out and provide for their families while women stayed home and nurtured their children. Now women have many more opportunities to share their unique gifts and talents with the larger world, while men have been invited to develop their capacity to be more nurturing and sensitive at home. Today, both men and women are often involved in providing for and nurturing their families.

Due to the cultural milieu present during Bible times, the feminine and motherly images for God are nowhere near as numerous in the Scriptures as are the masculine and fatherly images. However, the few that do exist can help expand our images and understandings of God. Included among the handful of mother images are Psalm 131:2; Isaiah 40:11, 49:15, and 66:13; Luke 15:8-10; and Matthew 23:37. Many other scripture passages speak of the tender, comforting, and nurturing actions of God that have been traditionally ascribed as feminine characteristics, such as those found in Hosea 11:3-4:

> Yet it was I who taught Ephraim to walk, I took them up in my arms . . . I led them with cords of human kindness, with bands of love. I was to them like those who lift infants to their cheeks. I bent down to them and fed them.

Jesus, who ignored cultural expectations and limitations by befriending and speaking with women about religious matters in public and by including them among his followers, embraced and activated both his masculine and feminine characteristics, traits that all of us need today in order to be whole. You might read the Gospels with an eye for how these complementary characteristics were evident in Jesus' life.

As you experiment with and expand your images and understandings of God, expect it to feel awkward at times. Spiritual growth sometimes calls us to leave what is safe and familiar, as Abraham and Sarah did, and venture into the land of risk-taking and unfamiliarity. If you have addressed God as "Father" all your life and have used the masculine pronouns "he" and "him," it might seem strange and uncomfortable to address God as "Mother" and use the feminine pronouns "she" and "her." You might consider trying it a couple times, and decide if using feminine images of God is helpful to you, both in how you image God and in how you pray to God. For example, by imaging God as mother, some of us might gain an *experiential* sense of God's tenderness and gentleness, which may have been missing when we relied solely upon the image of God as a father.

Other new images will probably not cause you to feel uncomfortable, such as that of "companion" or "friend." These, too, can help expand our understanding of God and open new pathways to prayer. Envisioning God as a friend may help us share more freely, openly, and honestly with God, just as we do with our other close friends. The Bible tells us that God is love (1 John 4:16), therefore whatever images we use should help us draw closer to our God of love and enhance our life of prayer.

Expectations of God and Prayer

So far we have looked at how we might choose to explore and expand our definition of prayer and have identified some tools with which we can add to our images of God. Now we turn our attention to the unrealistic and realistic expectations we may have of God and prayer, which, like our images of God, we often acquired in childhood.

Jesus tells us to be childlike, which is quite different from being childish. To be childlike is to trust in, rely upon, and be open to God just like young children are with their parents. On the other hand, when we are childish, our expectations of God and prayer tend to be unrealistic or immature. These unrealistic expectations reflect a lack of trust in, reliance upon, and openness to God. They are signs pointing to our reluctance to accept life as it is, our desire to control the events of our lives, or our feeble attempts to deny reality. Our approach to prayer becomes a frustrating one in which we demand to get what we want when we want it. Most of us can admit to having some childish or unrealistic expectations of God and prayer, so there is no need for shame or embarrassment. Instead, let's simply strive to let them go and replace them with childlike and realistic expectations that can liberate and lead us to a more satisfying prayer life.

Unrealistic and Realistic Expectations of God and Prayer

Unrealistic: God should respond immediately to my prayers.

Realistic: God responds to every prayer, but not always immediately. Many of our prayers take time to be answered, and we are called to wait with patient trust in God, confident that God will respond to us in the best possible way at the best possible time. (We'll look more closely at how prayers are answered in chapter 4.)

Unrealistic: God should suspend or reverse the laws of nature and of life and death when it affects me and the people I care about. In other words, if I pray for a loved one's health to be restored but he or she ends up dying, I might feel like God has let me down, doesn't care, or has even betrayed my trust.

Realistic: God is not likely to suspend or reverse the laws of nature, including the cycle of life and death, for you, me, or our loved ones. God will, however, be with us during these difficult times and provide us with the grace and strength to bear them.

Unrealistic: God should do whatever I tell God to do, like a personal genie or servant. God should give me exactly what I want when I want it.

Realistic: God's role is not to do whatever we ask or order. God sees the bigger picture of our individual lives and of our world, whereas our vision is quite limited. God is free to respond to us in the best possible way, which might be quite different from the "orders" and directions we give God in prayer. Again, our call is to have childlike trust in our divine parent.

Unrealistic: God should communicate more clearly with me.

Realistic: Perhaps God is a better communicator than we think, and our failure to hear God clearly may be because we do not know how God communicates, or we may have difficulty slowing and quieting down enough to hear God "speak" to us. (We'll address this issue in more detail in chapters 2 and 3.)

Unrealistic: God should solve my problems and the world's problems, even if neither I nor humanity as a whole puts forth sufficient effort and fails to cooperate with God.

Realistic: Prayer is a partnership and frequently the time we spend in prayer is meant to give us the inspiration, energy, and divine ideas to work with God toward reducing or solving some of our own personal problems as well as those of the world.

Pause, Ponder, or Practice

With which of the childish or unrealistic expectations can you relate? Which of the realistic expectations do you find appealing? Name any other unrealistic expectations you or many of us might have of God and prayer. How could they be changed to reflect a more realistic expectation?

Praying the Chapter

God of endless compassion and infinite understanding,
I have confined my prayer life by defining prayer too narrowly.
By constricting my images of you,
I have restricted my ability to sense your presence in my life.
I have misunderstood you because I have not sought
deeper and truer understandings of who you really are.
I have clung to unrealistic expectations of you because
realistic expectations sometimes require too much of me.

Help me to grow in my
understandings of what prayer is
and to expand my images
and understandings of who you are.

Teach me to pray from the heart,
with my whole being,
and with growing trust.

Heal me from misguided teachings
and any lingering hurts from childhood
that block my path to you.

Set me free from unrealistic and childish expectations,
for you are the Ground of Reality,
and it is in reality,
in the real stuff of my life,
and of this world,
that I will find
you.
Amen.

For Reflection, Journaling, or Discussion

1. Create your own personal definition of prayer, perhaps in two or three sentences, to help clarify what prayer means for you.

2. What are some of your favorite images of God? What images of God do you use when you pray? Do you think that adding to your God-images can add to or enhance your prayer life? Explain.

3. What are your thoughts and feelings about using feminine images of God, including the image of mother? Are you or is someone you know strongly opposed to using such images? Is it okay for people to use different images of God? Why or why not?

CHAPTER 2

GETTING STARTED

Let us deal a little with how this journey must begin; for the beginning is the most important part.
—Saint Teresa of Avila

STARTING OR RESTARTING OUR prayer life is easy to do, especially when we consider how eager God is to share a loving relationship with us. Like most new endeavors, such as an exercise program, it is most helpful to keep prayer simple and practical. In the same way that a person who wants to get in better shape sets some clear, attainable exercise goals, it can be helpful if we set some prayer goals that are well within our reach. For instance, we might have the goal to spend five minutes with God in prayer three days this week.

Goals and plans provide us with a sense of direction, which we need as much in prayer as we do in other aspects of our lives. Sometimes we drift away from prayer or have trouble getting started because we have neglected to make a concrete plan as to where, when, and how we will devote some time to prayer. When we do have such a plan in place, we have a much better chance of recharging our prayer life. And, as with other undertakings, when we have some "success" in prayer, it will, quite naturally, lead to more "success." We will find ourselves not only wanting to pray but actually taking the time to pray. Our resistance to prayer will lessen, and we will experience our personal power to get our prayer life restarted when we have lost our way.

No one has a perfect prayer life. I don't know anybody who would claim to be a good "pray-er," but I do know that many people would say they have a good prayer life—even though prayer has its inevitable difficulties and obstacles to overcome.

In this chapter, we will address one of the first and most powerful obstacles to prayer, that of pro-crastination. We will explore why we procrastinate when it comes to prayer, examine four inner resources or qualities we need to develop in order to foster our prayer relationship, and identify a five-step plan to help us get started again in prayer.

The Power of Procrastination

Perhaps most of us have wrestled with procrastination at one time or another. (For me, it is an ongoing wrestling match.) Those of us who would like to lose some weight, exercise, or improve our personal lives in some other way know how powerful procrastination can be. Some of us have encountered its power as we put off doing our taxes until the last minute or delay going to the doctor or dentist until it is absolutely necessary. In short, we tend to procrastinate doing those tasks that are unpleasant or difficult, that require more effort of us than we want to expend, or that are simply not as fun or satisfying as the alternatives.

But if we are honest with ourselves, we realize that our reasons for procrastinating are often quite flimsy and unreasonable—at least mine are. And in many cases, whatever we have put off doing must eventually be done. But you might be surprised and relieved to know that when it comes to prayer, the reasons we procrastinate are often very solid and reasonable! Rather than berating ourselves for putting off prayer, let's explore more closely some of the factors involved.

Why We Put Off Praying

We have so much to do. We are incredibly busy people with a multitude of tasks to do each day. We only have so much time and energy to spend, and life's daily demands seem to drain every last drop. We are often so active from the time we get up until the time we go to bed that prayer sometimes, quite unintentionally, gets squeezed out.

We find it difficult to slow and quiet down our racing minds in order to pray. Because we are so busy and our minds are so active, it can be very hard to slow down a bit in order for a meaningful prayer encounter to occur. For many of us, as soon as we sit down to pray, our thoughts speed up even more! One thought after another—often totally unrelated to prayer—races uncontrollably through our minds. And because our thoughts are so numerous and our minds are so unsettled, we may give up on trying to communicate with God. At such times, it can be as frustrating and fruitless to try to pray as it is to try to fall asleep when insomnia visits us.

We often intend to spend time with God but end up forgetting, or we try to pray at the end of the day when we are too exhausted to have any quality time with God. It's like going out to dinner with a friend when you are dead tired and can barely keep your eyes open. If we try to spend our most meaningful time with God when we are totally wiped-out, we set ourselves up to come away empty more times than not.

Our time spent in prayer is not satisfying. Many of our attempts to spend time with God in prayer have left us feeling dissatisfied, as if we somehow didn't really connect. It's similar to those times when we hope to enjoy some closeness with a friend or spouse, but some invisible barrier seems to block or prevent this from happening. The conversation seems forced rather than natural, or perhaps the other person doesn't appear to be too interested in what we have to say. Hence, we come away feeling more, rather than less, lonely. If we have consistently dissatisfying times with our friends and companions, we are either going to replace them or find some different ways to be together so that our relationships are more satisfying. The same is true of

God. If our time spent in prayer is not satisfying, we're either going to replace God with other activities or people, or we will need to discover some ways to develop a better connection.

Sometimes we get very discouraged and disappointed in prayer. We may have prayed very earnestly—even desperately—for something or someone, and it doesn't seem to have helped. We come away feeling very disappointed and may find ourselves wondering whether or not God even heard our prayers or cares about us at all! Prayers for a relationship to improve or for a loved one's health to be restored may seem to have gone unnoticed or unheard by the way they were answered—or not answered. In such situations, how can we not be discouraged? How can we not tend to turn away from God and prayer?

We may be confused about who God is and how prayer works. While we seldom get perfect clarity on the spiritual journey, feeling consistently confused or in the dark about some of the mysteries of faith can cause us to drift further and further away from God. For instance, many of us have wondered why God seemed to speak to people during biblical times but no longer appears to do so today. Or, we know that at any given moment millions of people are praying at the same time, so how can God possibly hear and respond to each of us in an intimate and personal way? Or how can God allow people to suffer in such horrible ways year after year, century after century, millennium after millennium? Questions such as these, if not adequately addressed, can make or break our prayer life and our faith.

Pause, Ponder, or Practice
Which of these reasons for putting off prayer do you relate to the most? What other factors, if any, cause you to procrastinate when it comes to prayer?

A Word of Hope

If you can relate to the power procrastination sometimes has on us and on our desire to pray, you have lots of company—including me! The good news is that there are some simple and effective ways to overcome procrastination and to get your prayer life restarted. We will look at them later in this chapter. And it is well within your personal power to experience more satisfaction in prayer, especially when you consider, as was mentioned earlier, the fact that God will help you! Rather than being one more task to add to your busy days, prayer can be a refreshing and renewing respite so that you will be able to call forth the inner energy to do all that you need to do. Distractions and racing thoughts can be tamed a bit so that prayer will become a truly meaningful time of connection with divine love.

Inner Resources We Need to Develop

It is human nature to want something for nothing—or for next to nothing. Perhaps that's one reason why so many people buy lottery tickets. The possibility of winning several million dollars for a one- or two-dollar investment sounds too good to be true, and, of course, it is for all but the lucky few. Sometimes, we complain about our prayer life—or lack of prayer life—despite knowing that we have put little time or energy into it. We want a big payoff—a quality prayer relationship—for a minimum investment on our part.

A more satisfying prayer life, a deeper relationship with God, is a gift God desires to give us. But this gift, which is always offered to us unconditionally, does not usually sustain itself once it is received without some significant reciprocal efforts on our part. Like most intimate relationships, especially the deepest and most enduring ones, our prayer relationship with God will be meaningful and satisfying as we develop and consistently call upon these four inner resources: desire, effort, commitment, and perseverance. Let's look at how these qualities can help us on our prayer journey to the heart of God.

Desire. The desire to pray is a yearning for God that God has placed within our hearts. The fact that you are reading a book such as this is a sign pointing to your desire for God and your desire for a meaningful relationship with God. The inner longing and hunger for God will help you—and me—hang in there when prayer periodically becomes empty, dry, or even arduous. Our God-given desire for closeness with God will also inspire us to return to prayer when we drift away or even when we quit praying for a period of time—no matter if our "sabbatical" is for a couple weeks or a couple decades.

Effort. Our relationship with God will require effort from us just as our other relationships do. We will need to do those things that foster and strengthen our friendship with God. First and foremost, we will need to put forth the effort of spending time with God on a regular basis, even during those periods in our life when we don't feel like it or when we are extraordinarily busy. Effort may also call us to learn more about prayer, to experiment with some different ways of praying, to seek advice from a spiritual director or pastor, or to try to pray when our hearts seem far away from God.

Commitment. Effort's twin is commitment. We will need to commit some regular time to prayer, just like we spend regular time eating, caring for our homes, and grocery shopping. If instead we pray only when we feel like it or when we are in need, it is unlikely that our relationship will be very satisfying. It would be similar to exercising only once every three or four weeks. Even though we feel good each time we exercise, if it is infrequent, we won't get in very good shape. We also tend to feel better after praying, even if we pray only once every month or two. But praying so sporadically does not get us in very good prayer shape nor does it tend to bring about the kind of relationship we want to have with God. For starters, I would suggest setting aside five or ten minutes for prayer at least three days each week.

Perseverance. At times, we will simply need to hang in there during the difficult moments we have in prayer. I have spent times praying when my mind just wouldn't settle down, as it flitted out of control from one unrelated thought to another. I come away from such prayer experiences—and I am hesitant to even label them as "prayer"—feeling like a complete failure as a pray-er. It is after these moments of feeling inept that I am most tempted to quit.

Perseverance is also needed when we question the efficacy of prayer, when we wonder whether or not we are just talking to ourselves, or when we even question God's existence. Instead of becoming overly discouraged when we face struggles and difficulties such as these, we must learn to accept that they are an inevitable part of our prayer journeys. Feeling discouraged, we may be tempted to quit, but we must persevere in the same way that a one-year-old child persists in her attempts to walk despite falling every few steps.

Pause, Ponder, or Practice

On a scale of 1 to 4 (1 = none, 2 = a little, 3 = a moderate amount, 4 = a lot), rate the strength of each of these four inner resources in you: desire, effort, commitment, and perseverance. What is your highest rating? What is your lowest?

Take a look at your lowest rating. This is one you will want to nurture the most. Your highest ratings are the strengths that will help you when you are most tempted to give up on prayer. Keep in mind that these may change. Your lowest rating today may one day be your highest.

Five Steps to Help Us Get Started in Prayer

✓**1. Decide where and when you will pray.** This step may seem rather obvious, but it is often overlooked. Sometimes we forget to pray or have a hard time getting our prayer lives restarted because we have not set aside a specific time and place to pray. We make plans to go out to lunch with a friend or colleague, but we haven't made concrete plans to have lunch with God.

While it is possible to pray anywhere and at any time, I would recommend that you identify where and when you would like to spend five or ten minutes with God—and only with God—as your main prayer times. It might be in the privacy of your home, perhaps in your bedroom. Or it may be easier to pray somewhere outside or in a secluded location at work. It is important to choose a relatively quiet place where you can be alone and are unlikely to be interrupted.

Think of this five- or ten-minute prayer time as the main meal you are going to have with God, whether it is three days each week or more than three days. Obviously, you and I can have many spontaneous "meals" or "snacks" throughout the day or week, but our main prayer "meals" are the ones we will focus on here.

Pause, Ponder, or Practice

For this week, beginning today if you would like, plan where and when you will spend five or ten minutes with God in prayer. Perhaps you will want to set a moderate goal of having three main meals with God this week rather than seven. (You can always have more than three, but achieving a goal of three prayer times helps us feel better about our progress than does setting a goal of seven and praying only five times.)

2. Get into a relaxed yet alert prayer posture. Most of us pay attention to our posture during a job interview or when applying for a bank loan, but we sometimes forget to do so when we are praying. We aren't trying to impress God with our "good" posture; instead, we are letting our bodies befriend us in prayer. While there are many prayer postures to choose from, I would like to suggest that you try one of these:

1) Sit up with your back straight (not stiff) and your feet flat on the floor. Place your open hands on your thighs, or place one cupped hand on your lap and rest your other cupped hand in it.

2) Lie down, perhaps on your bed, with pillows under your knees to flatten your lower back against the mattress and a pillow under your head. Place your interlaced fingers on your stomach or rest your hands by your sides.

3. Spend some time slowing and quieting down in preparation for prayer. Athletes know that by warming up gradually they reduce the risk of tearing or pulling a muscle in the midst of a game or contest. We pray-ers must do the opposite: slow down. Our minds tend to be filled with thoughts, whether we are just waking up, going to bed, or in the midst of our day. We need to spend a little time slowing down the speed and quantity of our thoughts in preparation for prayer. This is not easy to do at first, but with practice we will get better at it.

One way to do this is to take ten or more calming and cleansing breaths when you sit down or lie down to pray. Your stomach, more so than your chest, should extend slightly as you inhale and return to its normal position as you exhale. You might even choose to count these ten breaths on your fingers. In conjunction with your breathing, you could repeat a simple prayer phrase, such as one of these:

Breathe in	Breathe out
Loving God	slow me down
Gentle God	quiet my mind
Peace	be still
God grant me	peace

After ten breaths or combining your breaths with a prayer phrase, it is likely that your mind will still be quite active, and you may still be filled with many thoughts. Perhaps with additional practice and repetition of your prayer phrase, you will gradually become more quiet and calm within.

It is important to know and remember that our goal is not to become thought-less, but to lessen our thoughts, to slow them down, perhaps initially from seventy miles per hour to sixty. Just as athletes—and non-athletes, for that matter—gradually become more flexible and limber as a result of consistent stretching and warming up, we will become better at slowing and quieting down in preparation for prayer as we consistently practice this step. If we don't take a little bit of time to slow down, we are much more likely to pull a "prayer muscle," become agitated and restless, and give up on our attempts to spend time with God.

4. Pray a prayer of intention. Tell God that you intend to spend the next five or ten minutes in prayerful friendship. Again, this seems incredibly simple but it can be helpful to voice this intent and ask for God's help to spend a few minutes in prayer. Here are a few examples of prayers of intention:

- Creator God, I am here to spend time with you. Please help me not to run away.
- Loving God, the next five minutes are yours. I want to be with you.
- Comforting God, help me to be with you for the next few minutes. Teach me how to pray.
- God of endless compassion, I want to pray, yet I am so restless and easily distracted. Help me pray.

5. Pray in any way you want. Your time of preparation, of slowing and quieting down, blends naturally into prayer. You can choose from a variety of ways to spend the remaining minutes with God in loving friendship. You might just want to repeat your prayer phrase over and over and enjoy your peaceful time with God. Or you could pray the contents of your day and the plans you have for tomorrow. You might want to express gratitude, ask for forgiveness, or seek God's help with a problem or difficult relationship. Another possibility is to pray a prayer you know by heart, such as the Lord's Prayer or the twenty-third Psalm. You may also consider praying for someone else or just being with God in silent love. (We will look at some of these more closely in chapter 8.) Trust the Spirit of God to be with you and to help you pray in the ways that work best for you.

Praying the Chapter

Patient and persistent Creator,
Although you want to shower me with
countless blessings, I create many excuses
for not spending time with you.
Some of my reasons for procrastinating
are quite good; others are because I want
a relationship that requires little of me.

Increase my desire for you.
Help me put forth the reciprocal effort
that any important relationship needs,
for I know that none is more important
than the one I long to have with you.

Strengthen my commitment to prayer,
as you are always committed to me
in prayer and everywhere.

When I am discouraged and
tempted to quit praying,
help me persevere and
trust that you are near.

Teach me how to pray, O God.
Help me slow down my restless mind
in preparation for our special times together.
Inspire me to make a plan as to when
I will be with you, for I know
you are with me
always.
Amen.

For Reflection, Journaling, or Discussion

1. When is prayer most satisfying for you? Most dissatisfying? What factors contribute to feeling satisfied or dissatisfied?

2. Sometimes we resist prayer or quickly give up on praying because we have a hard time settling down and quieting our minds. Do you struggle with restlessness when you pray? Explain.

3. How have you progressed in your spiritual journey, including your life of prayer? In what areas would you like to make more progress?

CHAPTER 3

LISTENING FOR
GOD'S VOICE

*God not only speaks, but is, in a
sense, never silent. God's energy,
power, and voice never leave us.*
—Bill Huebsch

PRAYER CAN BE CHALLENGING
because it often seems like we are having a one-way
conversation with God. We can express our needs,
wants, complaints, and gratitude with precise verbal
clarity, but it seems like God's only response is continuous silence. Trying to believe that God is lovingly
and intimately involved in our lives—individually
and communally—when God seems to be silent, or
at least wordless, is difficult to say the least.

Despite the fact that God never seems to speak to
us, our human need for help from a power greater
than ourselves inspires us to continue speaking to
God—to continue entreating God with our heartfelt concerns. Frustrated because we have to do all
the talking, we may give up on prayer from time to
time only to experience a persistent inner urge that
leads us, like migratory birds, to return to our nest-
ing sight—the source of our origin.

While it is obvious that God does not tend to speak to us in a humanlike voice, we do believe that our God is a communicative God. Indeed, because God is God, then God is not only the Creator, but is also the Communicator. Instead of God being communication-challenged, we are invited and challenged to learn some of the many ways God communicates with us. God's communication style ranges from deepest subtlety and silence to rather overt pounding on our hearts or heads.

We can, however, stop insisting that God speak to us in the ways we want and begin listening and looking for other ways that God actually does speak to us. When we learn God's language, we discover that God is intimately and lovingly communicating with us. Our prayers are not offered to a distant God who is deaf and mute, but to a God who is near, to a God who hears, to a God who is right here with us at each moment.

God not only hears our every prayer, but God also speaks to us in, by, and through our life experiences. God may communicate by permeating us with the priceless gift of inner peace or through a friend who calls us at a time when we are most in need of a sympathetic ear. God might speak to us in a sunrise or sunset, in the bright eyes of a child, or through our tears, as well as in countless other ways.

In this chapter, we will identify some of the common ways God frequently communicates with people of prayer. We will also learn how to enhance our ability to "hear" God speaking to us in our daily lives. Hopefully, the frustration that is part of one-way prayer, of a monologue, will decrease, and the satisfaction that arises from two-way prayer, from a dialogue, will increase.

Toward a Two-way Relationship

Most of us have had the experience of being trapped in a conversation with someone who talked too much and listened too little. We wanted to share more of our thoughts with this person but had a hard time getting a word in edgewise. When this happens, we usually feel frustrated and eventually tune the person out. While the other person rambles on, we may nod our heads periodically and offer an obligatory "uh-huh" or two, but we are no longer really listening.

When you and I dominate the conversation with God, we are obviously going to have a hard time listening to and actually hearing God. If we talk all the time, how can God get a word in? Even when we dominate the conversation with God—and I've done it a lot in my life—God won't abandon us or tune us out; God is infinitely more tolerant and patient than we are. But God desires to communicate with us and longs for a two-way relationship. God wants to be heard just as we want to be heard. As we practice the art of listening, we might be surprised at how eager God is to speak to us. Maybe we'll be able to receive much more of what God desires to give us if we allow for some silent or quieter moments in our times spent in focused prayer.

Our tendency to over-talk might actually become a barrier to experiencing God's loving efforts to help us, just like a doctor would be limited in her ability to help a patient who never stopped talking and listened to what she had to say.

Pause, Ponder, or Practice

What characteristics does a good listener have? Which of these characteristics are well developed in you? Which are underdeveloped? Which of these characteristics could be helpful in your attempts to listen more closely to God?

Improving Our God-Listening Skills

Probably the great majority of us need to improve our listening skills, not only with God, but also with each other. What follows are six suggestions to help us listen more closely to God.

Strive for an attitude that expects God to communicate. If we don't expect God to communicate, we may lack the necessary openness and alertness with which to recognize God's multifaceted and subtle ways of speaking to us. However, when we begin adopting and nurturing an attitude that truly expects God to communicate with us, our hearts soften, and we become more alert and receptive to hearing God's voice.

✓ **It can be helpful to express to God your desire to listen and to have a two-way relationship.** Isn't it great when someone calls you and wants to talk with you? We can give God this same gift by expressing a desire to have a dialogue—not just a monologue—with God. We can also ask God to help us develop this type of mutual relationship in which we talk and listen, give and receive.

✓ **We can experiment with prayer postures and gestures which reflect our openness to receiving and hearing God's voice.** Perhaps the simplest gesture is to rest our hands on our thighs, palms up, or to hold out our hands in front of us or to the sides of us. Or we can use a repetitive circular motion with our hands to symbolically summon God's wisdom into our hearts and minds. Too often we neglect our bodies when praying and keep prayer tightly confined between our ears. Paradoxically, involving our bodies can actually open our ears and enable us to hear God's voice more clearly.

✓ **It can be helpful to begin our time in prayer by quieting and slowing down.** If we come to prayer agitated or stressed, it is going to be especially difficult to hear God's voice and to sense God's presence. Spending a minute or two focusing on our breathing or repeating a prayer phrase can help quiet us a bit and make two-way prayer more probable.

We need to allow for some silence in our lives, particularly in our times of prayer. This period of silence doesn't have to be long; in fact, it is often best to begin with periods as short as thirty or sixty seconds and gradually spend longer times as we get in "silence shape." To help ourselves quiet down, we might consider repeating a prayer phrase or a single word such as, "Loving God, I am listening" or "Speak to me" or "Peace."

Sometimes if we have a lot we want to share with God, it may be essential to unload it all into God's care before allowing for some silence. When we have a lot on our minds and are eager to talk to God, we will not be able to listen very well until we pour it all out. At times like these, it is almost impossible to have a dialogue with God until we have a monologue. I don't think God minds waiting for us to unload. Instead of running off after telling God all that is on our minds and in our hearts, we can spend a minute or two—or longer—just being with God. Having emptied ourselves, we can allow for some quieter time during which God can speak to us and refill us with abundant love and divine energy.

 Pause, Ponder, or Practice
How do you try to listen for God's voice in your life? Which of these six suggestions might help improve your God-listening skills?

Having looked at some ideas that may help improve our ability to hear God, let's consider some of the common ways God communicates with us.

Ten Common Ways God Communicates with Us

Through people. This may very well be God's most frequent way of communicating with us. Human beings are made in God's image and have the capacity to be like God: compassionate, loving, forgiving, creative, and so on. Because God's Spirit is within us, we can be a channel through which God speaks to others. When we offer words of support, encouragement, hope, forgiveness, and acceptance, God is often speaking through us. And when others offer these words to us, God is often speaking to us through them. The next time you are going through a difficult time and a friend offers some wise and healing words, perhaps you might sense God speaking to you through your friend.

Through the Bible. We can turn to the Bible to read words of comfort, forgiveness, correction, guidance, love . . . and hear God speaking to us in our own language. For example, we can turn to the book of Isaiah when we want to be comforted, to the book of James when we need to be challenged, to the book of Psalms when we desire to pray, and to the Gospels when we are seeking guidance. Whatever we choose to read in this vast library called the Bible, we need to approach God's word with a faith that truly expects to hear God's voice.

Through writings on spirituality. We are fortunate to live in a day and age in which we have access to the best spiritual writings from the saints and mystics of long ago who can guide us on our spiritual journeys. We are also living in a time when many excellent contemporary authors are sharing their spiritual insights with us. Whether we read something Julian of Norwich wrote in the fourteenth century or Henri Nouwen wrote in the twentieth century, God can, and often does, speak to us through these writings.

Through our own ideas that often come during or after spending some time in prayer. God has gifted us with the creative intelligence to solve many of our own problems. We can ask God for ideas on how to handle a difficult situation, a painful relationship, or a challenge at work and expect these ideas to arise within us. These ideas may come to you in the midst of your prayer, later in the day, the next day, or even days or weeks later. We will recognize God's voice in these ideas because they will tend to help us get unstuck, fill us with a sense of peace and purpose, and provide us with a sense of direction.

Through nature. It only takes a few moments and just a tiny bit of awareness to hear and see God speaking to us through so many aspects of creation: flowers, trees, sky, clouds, wind, and snow. Because so many of us live in urban areas, we need to reacquaint ourselves with God's presence in nature. We don't have to travel to a state or national park to see and hear God's voice in nature; God is also very much present in our plants and flower boxes, backyards (weeds and all), and neighborhood parks.

Through the arts. Throughout the ages, the human race has created, and continues to create, beautiful works of art. Paintings, sculptures, literature, dance, movies, and music abound with God's voice. And it is not just the "sacred" or "spiritual" works, such as Handel's *Messiah*, that echo God's voice, but the so-called "secular" works of art as well. God does not divide creation and creative works into categories of sacred and secular as we tend to do. Some of the most moving "secular" artworks—whether it be a novel, a painting, or a pop song—can sometimes fill us more deeply with a sense of God's presence, of God's voice, than a work that has been labeled "sacred" or "spiritual."

To what art forms are you drawn? In what ways do you like to create—writing, drawing, playing an instrument, singing, cross-stitching, gardening? Whether you are appreciating someone else's creative work or engaged in your own, listen for the voice of the Creator present in the arts.

Through church services. If we are attentive, participative, and prayerful, we will often hear God "speak" to us at church. God's voice might be in a reading that seems to be meant just for us, through the words of a song, in something the pastor or priest says, or when we receive Holy Communion. God's presence might also come to us in the parking lot when we exchange a hello with someone we know. Sometimes we are filled with a sense of God's peace when we are simply in the church building itself. At other times, the mere physical presence of those in attendance—many of whom we may not know—somehow strengthens a sense of God's spiritual presence in our lives.

Through spirituality and support groups. Twelve Step groups, grief groups, groups for the separated and divorced, Bible study groups, spirituality discussion groups, and prayer groups are filled with the voice of God. These smaller communities can often enable us to hear and sense God's presence very powerfully in our lives because they meet the needs of the particular life situations we find ourselves in. Consider seeking out a small spirituality group or support group to help you gain a deeper sense of God's presence and voice in your life.

Through journal writing. Many people who process their thoughts, problems, prayers, and life experiences in journals are amazed at how helpful it is. Writing tends to clarify our thoughts and help us probe them more deeply. And, as is frequently discovered, the solutions to many of our problems—and prayers—are lying just beneath the surface, waiting to be written. Whether we choose to write prayers addressed to God in our journals or just write our thoughts in the awareness of God's presence, God's voice often emerges and blends with our own. It's very much like the writing assignments we may have been given in English class. We might have felt stumped initially but, as we wrote, the assignments unfolded and took shape. God's voice may arise, unfold, and take shape within us as we give journal writing a chance—especially during those times when we are troubled, confused, or have a lot on our minds.

Through new beginnings. The Bible is filled with stories of people who experienced new beginnings. Jesus invited people to leave their old ways behind and start fresh. The same invitation is extended to you and me: let go of the pain of the past—whether it be our failures, mistakes, losses, or disappointments—and be open to beginning fresh this day, this moment. When we have a bad day or bad moment, the fact that we can begin again is a sign God is speaking to us. We might experience renewed hope, self-forgiveness, the grace to forgive someone else, a sense of courage, the energy to try again, or simply an intimation of God's unconditional love.

Pause, Ponder, or Practice
Which of these ten ways that God communicates with us have you experienced the most? Which would you like to experience more often? Explain.

Obviously, these are just a few ways many people of prayer have experienced God communing and communicating with them. We can be sure that God speaks in many other subtle, and often quite gentle, ways to all of us. However God chooses to communicate with you and me, we can count on God to consistently speak those words we can never hear too often—words of endless hope, unconditional love, and total acceptance.

Praying the Chapter

Loving and listening God,
I'm not very good at listening to those in my life whom
I can see and touch and who speak the same language I do,
much less listening for you, Spirit God,
who speaks in so many subtle ways.

Yet I believe that you—great as you are—
desire to speak intimately to me
and to be heard by me!
That, in and of itself,
is utterly amazing!
Rather than lamenting your silence,
help me to expect you to speak,
and to listen for your voice
within me and in all of creation.

Open the inner ear of my heart
and grant me the faith to recognize you
as the Great Communicator in the
everyday experiences of my life.

Show me how to be a little
more quiet, maybe even silent
once in a while,
so that I will not only hear your
continuous words of loving acceptance,
but speak these words to others
on your behalf.
Amen.

For Reflection, Journaling, or Discussion

1. God often communicates with us through other people. Recall some specific times in your life when someone's words or actions meant a great deal to you.

2. Sometimes it can be very helpful to write a letter to yourself in God's voice. Allow the indwelling Spirit of God to write you a letter of love, acceptance, encouragement, hope, or whatever God desires to say to you in this letter. You might also consider writing a dialogue between you and God or between you and Jesus.

3. Many spiritual advisors encourage us to listen to our own inner voice, to our own intuitions. How carefully do you listen to, honor, and act upon your inner voice and intuitions? Can we truly listen to God if we don't listen to ourselves? How can listening to God and listening to ourselves be complementary?

CHAPTER 4

ANSWERS TO PRAYER

We must learn that to expect God to do everything while we do nothing is not faith, but superstition.
—Martin Luther King Jr.

THE EXACT WAYS IN WHICH OUR prayers are answered is something no one knows. Just as a one-year-old child cannot understand what his or her parents' lives are all about, we cannot begin to comprehend what it is like to be God. As the years pass, children gain more knowledge about their parents, and we adults have the opportunity to learn more about God, including how God responds to prayer.

Still, a child of twelve or an adult of forty never has a complete understanding of his or her parents. And since God is God and we are not, the chasm between what we do know and what we don't know about our divine parent will always be vast. We need to accept our limitations when it comes to probing the mystery of how prayers are answered, yet at the same time remain open to the possibility of gaining some partial insights.

Fortunately, we don't need to have a perfect understanding of how prayers are answered in order to have a mutual relationship with God. I know next to nothing about how cars work, yet I am able to drive one and get to where I need to go. I trust that my car will not completely disintegrate as I drive down the freeway, although I am aware that mechanical breakdowns do happen periodically.

This analogy can be applied to our prayer lives: We are able to journey with God without knowing exactly how God is involved with our lives or the precise manner in which God responds to our prayers. When we have prayer breakdowns or difficulties, we can seek assistance from a number of God's mechanics—pastors, priests, spiritual directors, friends, retreats, books, tapes—in order to repair our prayer lives and get back on the road again. So while we are not able to know *everything* about how God answers prayers, the little bit we *can* know makes all the difference in the world. Having a healthy, albeit limited, understanding of how God responds to our prayers is of paramount importance if we are to grow in our prayer lives.

In this chapter we will look at what we need to keep in mind when approaching God with our prayer requests. We will also identify four broad ways that God responds to our prayers—ways that are very similar to how people respond positively to each other. Finally, we will look at those times when our prayers seem to go unanswered, including how angry we tend to feel toward God when the outcome we hoped and prayed for does not come about.

The Purpose of Prayer Is Not to Just Get Answers from God

When our primary goal in prayer is to get answers from God, we are like those people who seek our friendship primarily because of what they can get from us. We would prefer to be liked and valued and sought out for friendship because of who we are as individuals, rather than because others want something specific from us. True friends delight in giving and sharing with each other as a by-product of friendship—not as a primary goal.

Too often, we approach God with this desire to get something from God, as if God were a catalog from which we can order whatever we want. Or, as was mentioned in chapter 1, we subconsciously expect God to respond to our prayer requests in the same way a private servant or genie should. It's as if God were just sitting around unsure of what to do until we give God our next command or direction. Perhaps most of us, if we are honest with ourselves, can admit to having approached God this way—I know I sure have!

While God wants us to ask confidently for what we need and want, our relationship with God, like any other relationship, encompasses much more. A healthy, well-balanced prayer life certainly includes petitioning God, but it also includes prayers of intercession, gratitude, and awe. Being silently present to the mystery of God, as well as admitting our failings and asking for forgiveness, are also parts of a well-rounded prayer life.

Of course, it is human nature to become unbalanced in prayer, just as it is in other aspects of our lives. For example, we may get so caught up in our work that we don't spend as much time with our families as we would like. Or we may spend too much time responding to the needs and wants of family members and fail to take the necessary time to nurture ourselves.

When we recognize that we are out of balance, we can begin to take some simple steps to correct it. When our prayer lives have become ones in which we are only making requests of God and neglecting other aspects of prayer, we can take some simple steps to restore some balance to them. The point is we need to approach the art and mystery of prayer with more in mind than just getting the particular answers and responses we want. But because this chapter is about how God answers or responds to prayer, let's examine some ideas that may help us approach God confidently and with ever-deepening trust.

Toward a Better Understanding of How God Responds to Our Prayers

The answering of many of our prayers often involves partnership, requiring both God's efforts and our efforts. Sometimes, perhaps many times, we pray and then neglect to do our part to help bring about the answers or outcomes for which we hope. When we fail to take action, our prayers become more like wishes and tend to die without bearing fruit, or without bearing as much fruit as those times when we combine prayer with action.

One purpose of prayer is to help us tap into God's enormous power and love, so that we can respond in more creative and vibrant ways than if we rely solely upon our own limited power as human beings. For example, if we ask God to help us get along better with a coworker, but don't take any practical steps to heal the friction, such as suggesting lunch or a cup of coffee, then our prayer may not be answered as fully as we had hoped. Or if we are dissatisfied with the direction of our career paths and express our unhappiness to God in prayer, but neglect to seek out career counseling or refuse to explore the possibility of returning to school, our laments are not likely to lead to more satisfying work. So prayer is very much a partnership of the human with the divine. God does God's part, and we must do ours.

Pause, Ponder, or Practice

How does approaching prayer as a partnership empower the person who prays? What actions can you take to help answer some of the prayers you have at this point in time?

The answering of our prayers is a process, something that often takes place over a period of time. We are accustomed to getting what we need and want very quickly, from fast food to money from automated teller machines to information on the Internet. We tend to want God to respond just as quickly to our prayer requests and sometimes have difficulty accepting slower responses and answers. But the answering of many of our prayers is a process, sometimes a long one.

Our two previous examples—the prayer to get along better with a coworker and the prayer for more satisfying work—are likely to take some time to be answered. Perhaps what can help us be a little more patient is to discern if what we are requesting of God is likely to be answered in the very near future or if it will take a longer period of time. If it's going to require some time, we can pray for the patience to stay with the process and to recognize the mini-answers and steps of progress along the way.

Another example of a response to prayer that is likely to be a lengthy process is when we ask God to help us forgive someone. I have discovered that the passage of time is absolutely necessary in order for true forgiveness to take place. I am not able to forgive instantly, no matter how passionately I pray to be set free of my resentments, because time has not had a chance to fulfill its healing role.

We need to trust that God is intimately and lovingly involved in our lives, albeit in ways which are often hidden and unknown to us. Gardeners know they must wait for the seed to break open and for the roots to establish themselves before the first tender shoots will become visible. If they become impatient and take the planted seed out of the ground to check its progress, they interrupt the cycle of growth and risk killing the seed and the plant it could become.

With many of our prayer requests, God's activity and involvement is as hidden from us as planted seeds are from those who garden. Unlike gardeners who can usually expect to see the plant emerge within a week or so, we don't know how long it will be before we see any signs of how our prayers are turning out. When a response to prayer takes longer than we had planned, we may find ourselves questioning God's intimate involvement in our lives: What—if anything—is God doing and what could possibly be taking so long?! Does God truly care about my prayer, or is God involved with too many other important issues?

While it is true that many of our prayers are answered or responded to far more slowly than we would like, we can ask for the grace to continue to trust in God's loving concern for us. We might also pray for the strength to do what we can and for the grace to accept that we cannot know exactly what God is doing or how God is responding to us. We can affirm that something good—perhaps even surprising and completely different than what we had hoped for—is in the works. An example might be the person who is passed over for the promotion she is well-qualified for and desperately prays to get, only to receive an even better job opportunity a few months down the line.

Pause, Ponder, or Practice

Have you ever received a surprising response to any of your prayer requests? If so, how did the outcome surpass your initial hopes? What prayers of yours have taken a longer period of time to be answered than you would have liked?

We need to trust that God desires our good and struggles with us to bring something positive out of the most painful situations we face in life. We never question God more than when we face a senseless tragedy in life or some other painful situation, such as a serious illness. However, we must remember that the pain and suffering we experience in life is not something God causes, rather it is something God wants to help us through.

The mother whose child is killed by a drunk driver may decide to join MADD (Mothers Against Drunk Driving) when her grief has subsided a bit. This involvement does not bring back the life of her child, but it allows her to gradually transform her grief and anger into a life-giving force as she works with others to lobby various legislative bodies to enact tougher drunk driving laws. God helps her become a force for life, even though the precious and irreplaceable life she brought into this world was unjustly and violently snatched away from her. Again, God did not cause her child's death, but God is with her in her grief and desires to help her bring life to others—and to herself. We can look for ways that God is trying to bring something positive into our lives—even in the midst or aftermath of enormous pain and suffering. (We will look more closely at prayer and suffering in chapter 7.)

We need to look back in our own personal histories and recall how God has responded to our prayers in the past, so that we might more readily trust in God's providential care now and in the future. We tend to recognize God's presence in our lives in hindsight. In the midst of a challenging or painful situation, it is often very difficult to discern how God is providing for us. Or when we are experiencing a major life change, such as a new job or relocation to a new city, the accompanying stress makes it hard to be aware of God's companionate presence. But after the pain has subsided a bit or the challenging situation has been worked through, or after we have been at our new job for a while or have become somewhat settled in our new home, we can look back and often see some clear signs of how God journeyed with and provided for us.

Recognizing how God has helped us in the past strengthens our sense of trust in God's promise to be with us and provide for us now and in the future.

We need to accept that we are sometimes powerless to bring about the answers we want to some of our prayers. Admitting and accepting our powerlessness is not an easy thing to do; in fact, it's usually a last resort. The person who prays for her hurting marriage to improve, but whose husband refuses to join her in marriage counseling, will have to face her powerlessness. The same is true for the parents who pray for their teenage child whose life is being ruined by alcohol and drugs. Until their child is ready for help, a profound sense of powerlessness is going to be a part of their lives. In both of these examples, it will be necessary to bring these feelings of helplessness and powerlessness time and time again to God in prayer.

Perhaps because we are so accustomed to being independent and self-directed in many aspects of our lives, it is especially hard to accept the times when we are dependent upon the grace of God to sustain us in the midst of situations over which we have no power. Whether we are feeling powerless over our desire to change a coworker's negative attitude or about our heartfelt yearning to help those who are starving thousands of miles away, it doesn't take long to realize how little lies within our personal power to change many situations.

We are powerless over many—if not most—situations in our lives and in our world, but, paradoxically, when we can admit and accept our powerlessness, at least to some degree, we reclaim our God-given power to do what we can. We also receive the much-needed grace to let go and leave the remainder in God's tender care. In our powerlessness we can turn it over to a gracious God, and allow God to be our strength during a period in our lives when we are feeling most weak and helpless. Admitting, accepting, and praying our powerlessness helps us refocus our energies in a positive and creative direction, rather than spinning our wheels by trying to change those frustrating situations—and people—that lie outside the range of our personal power.

Pause, Ponder, or Practice

What situations have you prayed about in the past or are currently praying about that evoke a sense of powerlessness? Does admitting our powerlessness refute the belief that the answering of prayer often involves partnership? Why or why not?

Four Ways in Which God Responds to Every Prayer

When people respond positively to each other, they generally do so in one or more of these four ways: they listen to each other, talk to each other, do something for each other, or simply be with each other. God, too, responds to every one of our prayers in one or more of these four ways.

God listens to us. While listening to someone might seem to be rather passive, it is an act of caring and an active way of responding to each other. God is an active listener who cares about what we have asked or expressed in prayer. The fact that God listens to us with loving concern is, in and of itself, a powerful response to prayer.

It is analogous to those times when we share a painful experience with a friend. While our friends might not be able to do anything about our suffering, the fact that we are listened to and sympathized with is a response we really need. Our pain probably isn't completely gone, but sharing it with a friend who will listen to us with the ear of the heart helps to decrease its intensity. And when we pour out our hurts and desires to God's listening and empathetic ear, our pain may not be totally gone either. Perhaps we wish that God would do more for us, but we can take some solace in knowing that we were listened to by a friend who is deeply concerned for us, who is forever faithful, and who overflows with compassion.

God talks to us, communicates with us. When we talk over a problem with a friend who offers some sagely advice or encourages us, we feel a deep sense of appreciation for his or her words. God, too, talks to us in many ways, some of which we identified in chapter 3. God might speak an encouraging word through someone who compliments us just when our sense of self-worth is beginning to plunge. Or we might stumble upon a Bible verse that seems to be meant just for us, as it fills us with a renewed sense of hope. Among God's continuous words to us are:

"I love you always. I care about you and about what you ask of me in prayer. I always listen to you and am always willing to help you. Trust in my unconditional love for you and in my active involvement in your life."

God takes loving action on our behalf. How wonderful it is when friends and family members demonstrate how much we mean to them by the kind and thoughtful things they do for us! They remember our birthdays, care for us when we are sick, share a book with us, invite us to dinner, and send us e-mail just because they love us. Because God loves us passionately, God puts divine love into action in many, many ways. God's activity includes strengthening us, inspiring us with creative ideas, leading and guiding us, comforting us, forgiving us, and helping us through people and other aspects of creation. As was mentioned earlier, the exact ways that God helps us is unknown to us, but we *can* trust in our active God to take loving action on our behalf.

God is with us and will stay with us always.
Sometimes friends do not have to say anything to each other; they just enjoy being together. It's almost impossible for people to be with each other at every moment of their lives, but God is with you and me always. God will be with us and stay with us, even when we are powerless to change a situation we would desperately like to change. Of course, we don't always feel or sense that God is with us, but we can become more aware of God's presence by affirming this reality more often:

God is with me in the midst of my sadness.
God is with me and my mother as she lives her last days.
God is with me even though I just yelled at my kids again.
God is with me as I feel powerless to help those who are starving.
God is with me right now as I pray.
God is with me in my loneliness and in my desire for
  companionship.

So we can count on God to answer or respond to our prayers by listening, communicating, acting on our behalf, and by being with us always. We are God's very own children, and we are deeply loved by our compassionate God. We don't always get the responses we want to our prayers, and this is a reality we must struggle to accept again and again. We can and should pray with faith and hope for whatever is in our hearts and minds, but when our prayers are not answered in the ways we want, we can trust that God listened attentively to us, is with us always, and will help us and the people for whom we pray, but perhaps in ways we will never know or understand.

What Should We Do When We Don't Get the Responses We Want?

What we have just discussed regarding how God answers prayer is nice and neat on paper and in theory, but when it comes to real life it is often a messy and difficult process. It is especially difficult when we care deeply about something or someone. If I pray for God to heal a loved one who is dying, it is unlikely that I will calmly accept that death is part of life. I may also find it difficult to trust that God is really with me and my loved one. Instead, I might feel quite angry with God if this special person dies—especially if he or she is relatively young. I may also feel like God let me down, didn't listen to me, or doesn't even care about me. I might even feel like giving up on God and prayer for a while as I wrestle with my anger.

While we know in our minds some of the ways in which God answers our prayers, our hearts are not impressed with what our heads know and still often insist upon a particular response from God. And when we don't get this response, it is normal to feel angry with God. It's important to express your anger directly to God. We don't always have to be nice in prayer; Job and the psalmists taught us that we can rage against God! We can put God on trial and angrily hurl our questions at God:

Why did you allow my child to get killed by a drunk driver?!
Why won't you make my husband go to marriage counseling?!
Why did my child get involved with alcohol and drugs?!
Why do people die of starvation?!
Why did you let my loved one die before I was ready?!

God listens to questions such as these, and God will help you gain some insights and understanding over time. God will be with you as you try to accept the reality that some very unfair and painful things have happened to you in life, things that God never wanted you to suffer.

Hopefully, after we have poured out our anger to God and questioned God mercilessly, we can eventually—perhaps months or even a year or more later—get to the point of opening ourselves to God's tender mercy. God will respect our need for distance and run to embrace us when we are ready. Someday, perhaps, we will look back on this difficult and painful period and be able to see more clearly how God responded to our prayers. With the clarity of hindsight, we might come to realize that God was with us each and every step of the way, even though our pain and disappointment at the time prevented us from seeing and sensing God's loving presence.

Praying the chapter

God of unending mystery,
How I wish I knew your ways!
How I wish I knew exactly what happens
the moment I beseech you in prayer!
Gently free me from spending too much energy
wishing to know what I cannot know.
Help me to continue praying in the midst of
my perpetual unknowingness and to
trust in you, my divine parent,
who knows all, including
my deepest need.

I am honored to be
your partner, loving God.
Help me do my part, whenever I can,
to bring about creative responses to my prayers.
Strengthen my trust in your hidden
but active involvement in my life
and in the lives of those
for whom I pray.

Remind me to look back in my life
and recall how you have helped me in the
distant past and in the not-so-long ago,
so that I might trust you as I pray
in this present moment.

When my prayers are not answered
in the way I want, and I turn away
in anger and disappointment, please
do not turn away from me,
for I will come back
home to you
again.
Amen.

For Reflection, Journaling, or Discussion

1. What are some of your most powerful experiences of answered prayer? What are some of your most discouraging moments when your prayers seemed to go unanswered?

2. Do you think the level of our trust affects how God responds to our prayers? Why or why not? Do you usually trust God when you make a request in prayer? Explain.

3. Have you ever asked for something in prayer, but at a later date experienced gratitude because you didn't get what you had wanted? If so, explain.

CHAPTER 5

PRAYING WITH THE BIBLE

*Your word is a lamp to my feet
and a light to my path.*
                    —Psalm 119:105

IF WE KNEW WE WERE GOING TO BE stranded on a desert island for one year and could bring just two or three books with us, many of us might include the Bible among our selections. Some of us would choose the Bible simply because we have not read all of it, and now, trapped and isolated, we would certainly have more than enough time to read it through at least once. Perhaps the great majority of us would bring it along because we know how desperately we would need the strength and consolation of God's word in the midst of such a trying and lonely ordeal.

In the daily reality of life off the island, we also encounter difficulties and loneliness on a regular basis. When we struggle with a challenging situation or simply when we are hungry for God, we may turn to the Bible with the hope of drawing closer to the one who created us. Sometimes we experience this closeness and sometimes we don't. There are times when we can open the Bible almost at random and stumble upon a verse or passage that seems to be meant just for us at that particular moment. At other times, even when turning to a favorite story or verse, we come away totally empty.

Praying with the Bible, like all other ways of praying, cannot be forced or controlled by us. However, we *can* take a few practical, concrete steps to help foster more satisfying experiences. In this chapter, we will examine a few guidelines to help us pray with the Bible, explore some of the books and passages that are conducive to prayer, and discuss a handful of specific ways to pray with God's word. First, let's review some basic information about the Bible.

Bible Basics

The Bible consists of a collection of relatively short books, some less than one page in length, which were written during the span of more than a thousand years. The Bible contains sixty-six books in Protestant editions and seventy-three in Catholic editions and is more like a mini-library than a typical book we would read from front to back. Like any good library, the Bible includes a variety of literary forms such as poetry, myth, epic, legend, history, and parable, to name just a few. Obviously, when we read poetry, biblical or non-biblical, we do so with a different mindset than when we read history, biblical or non-biblical.

We also need to keep in mind that we don't share the same cultural experiences and worldview as the original biblical authors and their audiences. When we study the Bible, we need to be aware of both the context in which the individual books were written and the messages the divinely inspired authors were trying to convey to their communities, so that we too can find meaning in it for our lives. Without the guidance of biblical scholars, we risk misunderstanding or misinterpreting what God, through the human authors, intended to say. Even with the aid of biblical scholars, parts of the Bible can be incredibly hard to understand and, as many of us have discovered, some parts of the Bible are nearly impossible to pray with.

But while the Bible is a diverse and complex work, its messages are often incredibly simple and straightforward. It's hard to be much more clear and direct than "love one another as I have loved you" (John 15:12). We don't have to be biblical scholars or even read what they have to say about the Bible in order to pray with it; faith, trust in the Spirit's guidance, a modicum of Bible knowledge, and a few guidelines—which we will look at next—are all we need.

Praying with the Bible

We need to open the Bible with the expectation of encountering God's Word. When we read the Bible, we are not just reading any old book; we are reading *the* book. Perhaps because we have such easy access to Bibles (many of us own several), it is easy to unintentionally take it for granted. It wasn't many centuries ago when Bibles were extremely rare because they were copied by hand. In some cases, they were chained inside churches to prevent theft! So when we try to pray with the Bible, it can be helpful to remind ourselves that we are reading, meditating, and praying with the word of God.

Because the Bible is a book of faith, we need to approach it with faith. More than anything else, the Bible is meant to strengthen our faith and our relationship with God so that we might live more vibrantly as people of faith and respond more generously to the needs of others. The Bible is filled with stories of people who, like us, range from having no faith to possessing the deepest faith. Our faith, however fragile it might seem to be at any given moment, is strengthened, often imperceptibly, when we pray with the Bible.

It can be helpful to activate and apply our knowledge of the Bible when trying to pray with it. As was mentioned earlier, we don't need to be Bible experts in order to pray with the Bible, but it can be helpful at times to have just a little bit of knowledge about the different types of books and writings it contains. For instance, we will be able to pray more effectively with the short book of Jonah by remembering that the author is telling a story about the mercy and justice of God, not just an historical account of the life of Jonah. Praying with the story of Jonah and his reluctance to go to Nineveh can help us get in touch with our own reluctance to listen to and do the will of God. Or it might help us face the depth and intensity of our very human desires to have certain people—individuals or groups—punished rather than experience the grace of God's forgiveness. If we only read it as a factual and literal story, we may find ourselves wondering how Jonah survived in the belly of the fish for three days or focus on some other nonessential part of the story. We might also fail to see ourselves in the character of Jonah and perhaps neglect to pray for our own hearts to be softened and transformed, and thus continue our tendencies to judge and condemn others. Similarly, when we choose to pray with a selection from the Gospels, we can recall that the Spirit-inspired communities and authors were focusing on what was most important for them at that time, rather than rendering a purely bio-graphical account of Jesus' life.

Pause, Ponder, or Practice

How would you describe your knowledge of the Bible? With what books or styles of biblical writings are you most familiar? If you could sit down with a biblical scholar, what questions would you ask him or her?

Which Parts of the Bible Are Good to Use in Prayer?

Whether you have extensive knowledge of the Bible, are just becoming acquainted with it, or if your understanding lies somewhere in between, the following suggestions may help you discover—or rediscover—some meaningful verses, passages, or stories with which to pray.

Pray with the parts of the Bible with which you already have some familiarity. This might include Bible verses you have come to treasure or even learned by heart, stories you have heard in church, or ones you have read on your own. You might decide to pray with an entire book or with any part of the Bible you have become acquainted with thus far in your life. For example, perhaps you are familiar with the story of the Good Samaritan in the Gospel of Luke, or have been intrigued by the journey of Abraham and Sarah in the book of Genesis, or have been challenged—as I have—by the book of Jonah. Or maybe a particular verse such as "I can do all things through [Christ] who strengthens me" (Phil. 4:13) might be one that will enrich your time spent in prayer.

Pray with verses from the book of Proverbs. This book of the Bible is especially conducive to prayer because it is fairly easy to find individual verses that are rich in meaning. The wise sayings in Proverbs invite us to trust God, to be aware of how we are treating others, and to follow the path of wisdom in our daily lives. A verse such as "Trust in the Lord with all your heart, and do not rely on your own insight" (Prov. 3:5) serves as a simple, but much needed, reminder to trust God—something that is hard for many of us to do at times. The verse "Whoever belittles another lacks sense, but an intelligent person remains silent" (Prov. 11:12) confronts us when we have hurt another person with our words and challenges us to choose the much more difficult—and intelligent—path of silence. When praying with this verse, we might express regret for any destructive words we may have spoken, ask God for forgiveness, and pray for the courage to make amends. We might also ask God to help us pause and think so that silence might befriend us when we are tempted to speak impulsively and thoughtlessly.

Pray with the book of Psalms. Millions of people have discovered the beauty, power, and inexhaustible richness of the psalms. I keep coming across "new" psalms and discovering renewed meaning in ones that touched me years ago. The psalms are very accessible and prayer friendly like the proverbs. However, the book of Psalms is a collection of 150 songs and prayers, whereas the book of Proverbs is a collection of wise sayings.

Within many of these psalms, individual verses—oftentimes several verses of a particular psalm or an entire psalm—almost seem to leap off the page and exclaim, "Pray with me!" The power of the psalms has beckoned to people of prayer for thousands of years and continues to speak to our hearts today. They address the full spectrum of human existence, from life's angst-ridden moments to the times when joy is uncontainable.

As poetic songs, the book of Psalms is filled with powerful images to express the depth of human existence and of the constant faithfulness of God. Psalm 42, for example, includes the image of a deer longing for water to convey our deepest yearnings for God, while Psalm 23 centers upon the image of a shepherd to portray God's tender care for each one of us, especially as we walk through life's valleys.

Pray with verses from Isaiah, particularly from chapters 40-55. Biblical scholars tell us the book of Isaiah was written by at least three people. The second section of Isaiah, chapters 40–55, consists of some of the most beautiful verses in the Bible. Many of these verses, like those in the book of Psalms, are poetic in nature and are very conducive to prayer. The inspired writer tells of God's tremendous love for us and encourages us not to be afraid, as in the following passage:

You are precious in my sight, and honored, and I love you. . . .
Do not fear, for I am with you . . .
        —Isaiah 43: 4-5

Pray with the Gospels. The Gospels are among the best books in the Bible to use for prayer and meditation. The stories about Jesus, the stories and parables he told, and his teachings can be prayed and meditated with time and again. While the stories and teachings never change—and perhaps some are in danger of losing their transforming power because of over-familiarity—we change and bring new life experiences with us each time we visit them, just like we do when visiting a friend or relative. For example, we might discover new insights and applications for our lives when we pray and meditate with one of the stories about Jesus' birth (Matt. 1-2 or Luke 1-2:40), the parable of the sower (Mark 4:1-9, 13-20), or one of his teachings from the Sermon on the Mount (Matt. 5-7).

Pause, Ponder, or Practice

Take a few minutes and look through one or more of the Gospels. Make a mental or written note of some of the stories, parables, or teachings that you might consider praying with.

Pray with one or more of the New Testament epistles. If you do not already have your personal favorites, or if you are not too familiar with the New Testament epistles (letters), a good place to start might be with the book of James, Philippians, or 1 John. I have found the book of James to be among the easiest to understand and the hardest to live up to. As I pray and meditate with it, I am challenged to combine my faith with actions (no easy task), and to be more cognizant of the destructive potential of my words. I am encouraged and empowered by some of the passages in Philippians, while 1 John reminds me that God is love and calls me to continue my efforts to love others no matter how many times I fail.

Eight Ways to Pray with the Bible

Having identified some parts of the Bible that may be helpful to pray with, let's now look at some specific ways we can actually pray with our scripture selections. In our Christian tradition, the ancient practice of Lectio (pronounced *leksio*) Divina serves as a time-proven way to pray with the Bible. Lectio Divina is a way of praying with God's word that involves reading, meditating, praying, and contemplating. These four steps may be sequential or blend together as the Spirit guides us. You might keep them in mind as you consider some of the following eight ways of praying with the Bible.

1. Use a Bible passage to help you enter the doorway of prayer and as a way to get started. Sometimes when we try to pray, we are so unsettled and so caught up in the affairs of daily life that we have a hard time focusing our attention on our friendship with God. Taking a few moments to read something from the Bible can help us redirect our attention toward God. The part of the Bible we select—whether it be a single verse or a longer passage—is meant to help us turn our hearts and minds toward God and set a prayerful ambiance or tone. For example, we could read Psalm 23 once or twice to help us slow down and cross the threshold of prayer. Once our scripture selection has launched us into prayer, we let it go. Having crossed the doorway of prayer, we pray in whatever way we need to at that moment. The scripture selection has served its simple but important purpose of getting us started, which is sometimes the hardest thing to do when it comes to prayer.

2. Focus on the contents of the Scripture passage and allow it to steer your time spent in prayer. When we make a scripture selection the focus of our prayer, we are deciding to meditate upon it and apply it to our lives. Unlike the previous suggestion, which is meant to launch us into prayer, focusing on a particular passage from the Bible is intended to be the substance of our prayer. The words of scripture, which speak to us at this moment in time, steer the direction of our prayer and inspire its content. For instance, we could decide to make Psalm 23 the substance of our prayer experience. As we slowly read this psalm, the phrase within verse four, "you are with me," might be the one that catches our eyes—and hearts. Perhaps we are going through a challenging time and need to be reassured of God's presence. So we might just zero in on this short phrase and make it the center of our prayer experience. We could prayerfully repeat the phrase, "you are with me," over and over, or simply ask God to be with us in the midst of our worries about the near or distant future.

3. Pray with passages from the Bible that attract you. The words in the Bible that speak of God's comfort, encouragement, forgiveness, love, and acceptance can never be absorbed deeply enough. The fact is we are fragile human beings who live in a world that is often quite frightening and troubling. Inner and outer storms are part of life, so we turn to God's word to help quiet our fears and increase our trust in God. Our gentle God desires to console, guide, inspire, heal, and help us as we pray and meditate with scripture passages that attract us, such as:

Do not fear, for I am with you, do not be afraid, for I am your God; I will strengthen you, I will help you, I will uphold you . . .
—Isaiah 41:10

4. Pray with passages from the Bible that challenge you, turn you off, or that you resist. When we veer off course and gravitate toward the lower and lesser paths in life, God's word can confront, challenge, and correct us. Some of the words in the Bible, if we don't run from them, help us get back on the right track and lead us along the much more rewarding higher road. In the aftermath of an angry exchange with a fellow wounded traveler, spending time in prayer with the following verse confronts us with how our words exacerbated the conflict and inspires us to try to do it differently in the future:

A soft answer turns away wrath, but a harsh word stirs up anger.
—Proverbs 15:1

An example of another passage we might find ourselves initially resisting is the story in which the widow gives away all she has to live on (Mark 12: 41-44). Her generosity confronts us with the careful and controlled way we may sometimes give of our precious time, unique talents, and abundant resources. Or Jesus' command to not judge (Matt. 7:1) can stop us in our tracks when we have begun to take another person's inventory and steer us back toward the path of unconditional acceptance.

5. Slowly and prayerfully read a single verse or a relatively short passage two or three times. If possible, read it aloud at least once. When it comes to praying with the Bible, reading slowly—perhaps twice as slowly as we normally do—is an effective way to foster a more meaningful encounter with God. Reading a single verse or short passage more than once can be especially advantageous, because we often pick up on a word, phrase, or nuance we may have missed the first time through. When reading a scripture verse or passage two or more times, we might pause for fifteen seconds, a half minute, or longer before reading it again and allow God's word to sink deeply into our hearts and minds. If your setting allows you to read aloud, you benefit from hearing the words as well as seeing them. This is an especially good way to pray when we don't have anything particular to talk to God about, so we let God talk to us.

Pause, Ponder, or Practice
Slowly and prayerfully read the following verse (or another verse of your choosing) two or three times or more. Allow for a brief period of silence between each reading and just bask in God's word. If possible, read it aloud at least once.

And when you turn to the right or when you turn to the left, your ears shall hear a word behind you, saying, "This is the way; walk in it."
   —Isaiah 30:21

6. Try paraphrasing or altering the verse or passage you have selected for your prayer so that it has more personal meaning for you. If you are reticent to change the words of the Bible, keep in mind that our only purpose for doing so is to help us draw closer to God. You might even be pleasantly surprised by how much it can enhance your prayer. For example, by simply adding your name in the following verse, you might find it to be more personally meaningful:

(Your name), be strong and courageous; do not be frightened or dismayed, for the Lord your God is with you, (your name), wherever you go.
   —Joshua 1:9

Or we could rewrite the twenty-third Psalm so that it speaks more poignantly to the circumstances of our lives today . . .

The Creator is my constant guide; I shall never be lost. God graciously leads and surprises me each day of my life's journey. Knowing how needy I am, the Tender One supports me and surrounds me with caring companions who treasure me . . .

7. As you pray, enter the scripture passage and allow it to enter you as you apply it to your life. We might do so by imagining that we are one of the characters in a particular Bible story, perhaps the older son in the parable of the "Prodigal Son" (Luke 15). As the older son (daughter), we might complain about how unfair life or God has been with us. Or when we pray with the story of Joseph and his brothers (Genesis 37-50), we might share our wounds with God and ask for the willingness to eventually forgive those who have hurt us, just as Joseph forgave his brothers for selling him into slavery. The verse from Joshua that we looked at a moment ago might easily be applied to our lives when we are in the midst of a disorienting experience, such as the upheaval of a move, a painful separation, or the illness of an aging parent.

8. Record some of your favorite Bible verses in a notebook or journal and pray with one or more of them when the need or desire arises. Because the Bible is such an enormous work, it can be helpful to record some of the verses we have found to be most meaningful, so that we can easily locate them and pray with them. Like restaurant owners, we might create a menu of Bible verses from which we can make our selections. Some days we might be hungry for a comforting word and other days we might be craving some guidance.

I have recorded hundreds of verses in a journal, and sometimes during my prayer I slowly read ten or twenty of them. At other times, I read through these verses and zero in on the one that seems to be most helpful to me at that moment in my life. On tough days or when I am feeling especially vulnerable, I write one down on a slip of paper, stick it in my pocket, and carry it—and allow it to carry me—throughout the day. And at other times, I commit a verse or part of a verse to memory and use it to help me remember God's intimate presence in my life.

Praying with the Bible, as with all ways of praying, is not a matter of mastering any particular technique. Rather, it is simply a matter of opening our hearts to the one who desires intimacy, to the one whose heart is filled with unconditional love for you and me. And oftentimes God's passionate love can be experienced more profoundly as we creatively pray and meditate with the Creator's words in the Holy Bible.

Praying the Chapter

> Word of Life,
> I hunger for your
> life-giving words in the Bible.
> I long to draw closer to you by
> praying with your holy word,
> but sometimes the content confuses
> me and the volume overwhelms me.
>
> Thank you for the biblical scholars
> whose dedicated work helps me,
> and other people of faith as well,
> gain more understanding.

Thank you, too, for making your word
so simple and clear that I don't
need to be a scripture scholar in order
to pray with it. All I need to be is
a person of faith.

Help me to not let my desire
to understand the Bible more clearly
stop me from praying with it.
Reveal to me the passages
that can befriend me in prayer.
I know they are there and that
you will lead me to them,
and through them
lead me to you.
Amen.

For Reflection, Journaling, or Discussion

1. If you were to take a few minutes right now to
pray with the Bible, which passage would you select?
Why? If a friend of yours were going through a difficult time and asked for your help in finding Bible passages to pray with, what suggestions would you make?

2. What are some of your favorite psalms? If you
are not familiar with the book of Psalms, glance
through a couple and see if some of the verses have
any prayer appeal.

3. What information or suggestions from this
chapter might be helpful to you as you pray with
the Bible?

CHAPTER 6

RESTING IN GOD

The best prayer is to rest in the goodness of God, knowing that that goodness can reach right down to our lowest depths of need.
—Julian of Norwich

I READ IN A NEWSPAPER ARTICLE THAT most of us are not getting sufficient rest these days. Whether you are just beginning to establish yourself in the world or have been around for a while, you may long for more rest than you are currently experiencing. If you are a parent—single or married—and have children who are very young, about to be launched from the family nest, or somewhere in between, you probably have become intimately acquainted with exhaustion. Because we have so much going on each day, because we are pulled in so many directions and have a multitude of responsibilities to fulfill at home and at work, our whole person—body, mind, emotions, and spirit—suffers from a lack of wholeness due to insufficient rest.

As some of us have painfully discovered, banks charge a significant fee when a check is returned for "non-sufficient funds." But that financial penalty pales in comparison to the price we pay as human beings for overdrawing our physical, emotional, and spiritual accounts and failing to replenish them with the rest we need. How many times at work or at home have we said or heard someone else joyfully exclaim, "I'm really feeling well-rested and refreshed"? I suspect that most of us—along with our friends, coworkers, and family—tend to lament how tired we feel. I know I am not alone in feeling very tired by Tuesday, exhausted by Thursday, and wiped-out by Friday on a weekly basis.

The fact is we are under-rested as individuals and as a society. It has become such a significant problem that a name has been given for its extreme manifestation: chronic fatigue syndrome. Many of us who are frequently tired feel like the possibility of obtaining more rest is, in the real circumstances of our lives, an impossibility. We have accepted tiredness and fatigue as part of life and have given our personal power away. Seduced by the incessant cultural call to "do-ism" and "busy-ism," we have lost our sense of personal choice regarding our fundamental need for rest. Not only are we lacking the rest we need, in its void we are experiencing a growing sense of restlessness and boredom, and we are hungering for something we can't quite place our fingers on.

This chapter is about reclaiming our power to seek out the interconnected and interdependent physical, emotional, and spiritual rest we need so that we can be truly whole. We will explore some of the signs that indicate we need more rest, learn how the Bible encourages us to take time for rest, and identify some practical ways to recharge our "batteries." Special attention will be given to how we might begin to rest in God and allow ourselves to be loved, nurtured, and simply be—rather than do. Our God desires that we be good to ourselves by listening to and fulfilling our need for rest.

The Rhythm of Life

Working hard is necessary in many aspects of life, for we all know that success doesn't usually just fall into our laps. Our culture rewards and praises those who work and study hard and, when we receive such praise, it inspires us to put forth even more effort! More than likely, most of us have not been complimented or praised for resting, unless we were sick.

Recent studies are beginning to show, however, that those who spend more and more hours working at their jobs are not as effective or productive as those who work hard but also take the time to rest and play—and, I would add, pray. Those who live more balanced lives seem to be just as successful, sometimes even more so, than those who just increase the amount of time spent working. We reach a point when the time we spend working becomes increasingly unproductive, no matter how hard we may drive ourselves.

Life has a definite rhythm to it: day and night, summer and winter, work and play, activity and rest. Our challenge is to listen to, honor, and consciously choose to live out all sides of the rhythmic dance, rather than discounting and neglecting our basic need for rest. This calls us to make a counter-cultural choice each day, to say no to societal voices that entice us to engage in more and more activity at the expense of the refreshing and renewing rest we need.

Because of electricity, we can—and do—light up the darkness of night, whereas ancient peoples, including people in the Bible, had to stop their activities at night and rest. They *had* to honor nature's rhythm, but we must *choose* to do so. And, deep inside, we know that nature can show us a better way. If it were light all the time, the natural world would be out of balance. Plants and animals need the dark and so do we. As a part of nature, we cannot do without the rest and peacefulness that all of creation needs.

Pause, Ponder, or Practice
Are you in need of more rest? Has your life become increasingly busy? If so, what is requiring more of your time? What changes could you make in your schedule in order to get more rest?

The Saving Grace of Resting in God

Life takes a toll on us. We only have so much energy to spend during the course of our earthly pilgrimage. Not getting enough physical rest is only one energy-robber; there are many others: grief, loneliness, personal problems, concerns about loved ones, fears of violence, a sense of being disconnected, feeling powerless and helpless over the world's brokenness, and worries about the near or distant future are experienced by many of us.

While we are responsible for dealing with our own problems, we don't have to do so alone. We can turn to each other for help, and we can turn to our ever-present companion who desires to give us a helping hand and who wants us to let go of life's burdens for a while. When we let God hold us and our problems for a period of time and just rest in God's love, we come away more refreshed and with the grace-filled awareness that God is with us and is helping us in life! Our problems don't magically go away, but they tend to feel a little lighter and more manageable as a result of sharing them with God—as a result of letting God be our strength. Oftentimes we regain a sense of perspective or discover a way to resolve a situation that may have previously baffled us. Let's look at some common signs that indicate our need to take a little time apart to rest in God.

We Need to Rest in God When . . .

We feel overwhelmed. When we are feeling overwhelmed, we feel loaded down, covered, or buried by our responsibilities, problems, and activities. We feel like we don't have enough time to do all that needs to be done, much less "waste" any of our precious time resting of all things! We may feel so overwhelmed, we don't even know where to start, and thus we fall prey to worry, which only makes everything seem even more overwhelming. It becomes a vicious cycle with no end in sight.

We feel exhausted. We feel drained, worn out, fatigued, like we can't go another step. This is a sign pointing to our need for both physical and spiritual rest. The daily grind has ground us down. Our inner gas tanks are on empty, and we need to refill in order to fulfill our responsibilities. Like a driver who must abandon his car because he keeps driving with the needle on empty, we end up abandoning and mistreating ourselves—and oftentimes others as well—when we continue to push ourselves long after our energy tanks have become empty.

We feel consumed with worries, fears, or remorse. To be consumed means to be used up, expended, destroyed, or eaten up. Sometimes our worries, fears, and feelings of remorse consume us. They circulate around and around, over and over in our minds. We may even feel powerless to redirect our thoughts in a more positive and life-generating direction. Unable to free ourselves, we suffer emotional and spiritual fatigue as a result.

We feel anxious. Anxiety is a gnawing feeling of apprehension and dis-ease. A synonym of anxiety is worry, but it is a worry that may be attached to something specific, such as a forthcoming medical exam, or it may be a general feeling of anxiety that doesn't seem to point to anything specific. Sometimes anxiety can penetrate us so deeply and become such a frequent visitor, we feel powerless to rid ourselves of its discomfort. It tends to rob us of the inner peace and sense of personal power our God desires for us.

We feel crabby, irritable, angry, and frustrated. We experience these feelings even when we are well-rested, and they are perfectly okay feelings to have. We may be in need of physical, emotional, or spiritual rest, however, if they are surfacing more frequently or with more intensity than usual or if we are expressing them in poor and reactionary ways.

We feel bored or restless. We may be in need of rest when life seems dull or when we want to do something to escape feelings of boredom for a while. Usually when we choose an activity with the motive of escaping, even if it is a healthy activity such as reading a book or going to a movie, we tend to still feel bored and dissatisfied afterwards. But when we make a thorough probe into the origins of these bored and restless feelings, we can assess our needs more accurately and make a more creative choice. Perhaps a movie is just what we need in order to relax a bit, or perhaps we need to allow God to hold us for a while—or both. The point is we can let our restlessness and boredom drive us away from or to the God who desires to help us rediscover rest and assist us in making good choices for ourselves.

Pause, Ponder, or Practice

Which of these six signs pointing to our need for rest do you experience the most? Ask a friend, companion, or spouse which signs are most indicative of his or her need for rest.

The Bible Encourages Us to Rest

God knows our human need for rest, especially if we are going to live positive and creative lives. Many passages in the Bible, of which the following are just a sample, encourage us to seek out the physical, emotional, and spiritual rest we need.

And on the seventh day God finished the work . . . and rested . . . (Gen. 2:2)
Notice how according to this creation story even God stops working and rests! We have to make a choice to stop all our activities for a period of time—for ten minutes, an hour, half a day, or longer—and take the rest we need. Rest is always offered to us, but we must choose to accept it.

[God] makes me lie down in green pastures; [God] leads me beside still waters; [God] restores my soul . . . (Psalms 23:2-3)
In this passage the psalmist uses a beautiful and appealing summer image of lying down on green grass next to a lake or stream to inspire us to seek out the rest God desires to share with us.

My soul rests in God alone, from whom comes my salvation (Psalms 62:1 NAB)

God alone is the one who can give us the type of rest that no one and nothing else can. When we rest in God, we are quite literally saved—from being crabby or short with people, from making poor choices, from quitting or giving up, from getting too down on ourselves or others, and so on.

In the morning, while it was still very dark, [Jesus] got up and went out to a deserted place, and there he prayed. (Mark 1:35)

In this passage, Jesus sacrifices the physical rest of sleep and opts for the spiritual rest of communing with God. He took time for the rest that comes from prayer. I doubt that many of us are any busier than Jesus was during his public ministry. We can't make time for prayer, as there are only twenty-four hours in a day. Instead, we need to *take* time to be alone with God in restful prayer as Jesus did.

"Come to me, all you that are weary and are carrying heavy burdens, and I will give you rest." (Matt. 11:28)

Jesus invites us to stop our work, stop our activities, and lay down the heavy loads we are carrying. We are promised the gift of regenerating rest, if we will only take some time—perhaps just a few minutes—and allow our loving God to shoulder a portion of our load.

Ten Ways to Prayerfully Rest in and with God

1. When feeling overwhelmed, it can be helpful to write down all that is going on in your life and share this list with God in prayer. It is not only cathartic to write it down on paper, but we are also able to see more clearly exactly what is going on in our lives. Our list may include daily tasks such as laundry, dishes, and transporting the kids to one of their many activities. It might also include our responsibilities at work, difficulties with a boss or coworker, and any rapidly approaching deadlines we are concerned about. We might also name what is going on inside us—our thoughts, worries, regrets, health concerns, or emotional state. We may choose to circle those two or three items that are most overwhelming or burdensome to us and share these with God in prayer. We can bring anything and everything to God in prayer, no matter how insignificant or trivial we may think it is in the grand scheme of things, for God desires to help us in the details of our daily lives. Neither we nor any of our problems and concerns are insignificant to God.

2. Lie down with a pillow under your head and a couple pillows under your knees (which flattens your lower back). Place your list from suggestion #1 on your chest, and allow God to hold it—and you—for a while. By taking our hands off the list, we are symbolically allowing God to hold it for a while. Placing it near our hearts, we let our lists rise and fall with each relaxing breath, knowing that

God is in our spiritual hearts. We may have to resist some initial urges to get up and accomplish something on our lists, much like a parent who helps her resistant child settle in for an afternoon nap.

As we lie there, we might repeat a short prayer phrase such as "Lord, help me" or breathe in and out "God's peace." Or when we are really stressed and stretched, we might feel the heaviness of all that we have to do and cry out "I can't take it anymore!" We may lie there in quiet communion with God, perhaps just focusing on our breathing, or we may need to pour out the contents of our hearts with a barrage of words. After a period of time, perhaps just ten or twenty minutes, we may gain some insights regarding what we need to do next. Taking some time to let go and rest in God often helps us discern what needs to be done in the near future and what can be postponed until a later date.

3. Write down one or two things that are especially difficult or draining for you on a slip of paper and place it in your Bible next to a favorite scripture passage or in a God box or God can. For instance, you might choose to place the slip of paper next to Matthew 11:28, "Come to me, all you that are weary and are carrying heavy burdens, and I will give you rest." Or you could place it in a God box or God can, which represents giving our concern over to God's care. We might choose to decorate the box or can (shoe boxes and coffee cans work great) so that it looks more attractive and spiritual. Then we cut a slit in its lid large enough for a folded piece of paper to fit through.

Dropping our slips of paper in the Bible, God box, or God can is a symbolic act—a way to ritually and physically turn it over, a way of letting go. It helps to strengthen our trust in God's intimate and active presence, and whenever our trust in God is renewed and strengthened, our load is reduced and lightened. I have found this simple way of praying to be especially liberating when I am bound by worries or stuck in relentless remorse over my failures. Not too long after I have placed my prayer in my Bible, my God box, or my God can, the intensity of my worry or remorse has reduced significantly.

4. Pray an affirmation over and over. Let the bed you lie on or the chair you sit on symbolize how God is holding and supporting you. Affirmations are positive statements that reduce our feelings of being powerless and overwhelmed, and help us regain a sense of personal power. As we repeat affirmations over and over, the words sink deeper within us and calm the inner chaos. Both the words themselves and the repetition are soothing. As we physically relax and let our bodies sink into the chair or bed, we imagine God holding and supporting us just as securely. Here are a few sample affirmations:

• God is with me.
• God is helping me with (name the situation).
• I choose to let go and rest in God.
• Everything will be okay.
• I embrace God's peace.
• God is holding and helping me.

Pause, Ponder, or Practice

Consider writing five or ten additional affirmations that could be used in prayer. Try praying with one or more of these affirmations for a couple days and discern whether or not this is a helpful way for you to rest in God's peaceful presence.

5. Pray Reinhold Niebuhr's "Serenity Prayer": "God grant me the serenity to accept the things I cannot change, the courage to change the things I can, and the wisdom to know the difference."

So much of life lies outside our personal control, and we often become tired, stressed, or obsessed when we try to control or change what we cannot. Many people, particularly those in Twelve Step programs, have found this prayer to be a lifeline to inner peace. You might choose to repeat it over and over when you are in need of God's peace and rest. Or you could consider personalizing the prayer by applying it to a specific situation as in the italic print below.

- God grant me the serenity to accept the things I cannot change, *like the fact that I said something hurtful to my wife yesterday when we were arguing. Although I wish I hadn't said those words, I did speak them.*

- The courage to change the things I can, *I can apologize and ask for forgiveness.*

- And the wisdom to know the difference. *I will own my behavior, apologize, ask for forgiveness, forgive myself, and try to do better the next time we argue.*

6. Hold something that has spiritual significance for you as a reminder that God is holding you. For example, this might be a Bible, a small cross, a picture, a rock or shell you picked up on vacation, a Twelve Step medallion, or a carving. As we lovingly hold this object, we include the much-neglected sense of touch in our prayer, and prayerfully imagine God holding us and filling us with restful inner peace.

7. Go for a walk and talk with God. Sometimes when we go for a walk, our stress dissipates, we feel less overwhelmed, and we gain more clarity of thought. We might choose to share a particular problem with God as we walk or just repeat a prayer phrase or affirmation over and over, such as "God is with me." Simply getting outside is very refreshing and regenerating, especially if we have been cooped up for a while. Also, the movement and rhythm of walking is often relaxing in itself.

8. Spend some time in nature observing the natural world. Jesus invites us to "look at the birds of the air" and to "consider the lilies of the field" (Matt. 6: 26, 28) as an antidote to worry and as a reminder that God is providing for us. Sometimes just pausing to feel the grass beneath our feet, perhaps even sitting or lying down on the grass, can be a soothing balm for our restless bodies and spirits.

9. Enjoy someone else's artwork or create your own. Music, paintings, novels, theater, and movies are part of God's ongoing creation. Perhaps sinking into a good novel or being carried away by a favorite CD or strolling leisurely through an art gallery may help refresh your weary soul. Or even if you draw as poorly as I do, you might consider enrolling in a drawing class. Perhaps you've always wanted to learn to play a musical instrument or participate in a book discussion group. Doing so helps us stay in balance, and being in balance is conducive to feeling more rested and energetic.

10. Play. Just as God appreciates us when we are responsible and responsive to others, God also delights in us when we let go of our responsibilities for a period of time and respond to God's invitation to enjoy life, to laugh, relax, and play. Only one letter is different in the words "play" and "pray," and perhaps they are more closely related and interdependent than we think. When we pray and trust God, we are set free to play wholeheartedly, without guilt's shadow hovering and telling us that we should be doing something more productive. When we take time to play, we are letting go and trusting that God will continue to help us with the more serious stuff that is a part of our lives.

Praying the Chapter

God of rest,
How I long to rest in you, yet I resist
surrendering to your tender care out of
the illusion that I am self-sufficient.
I find that it is much more comfortable
to do, to stay busy, to take on more and more,

and continue to complain about how tired I am,
than it is take the necessary time
to rest my body, mind, and spirit.
You see, that way I can stay
in control, in charge, on top of things,
and avoid feeling—God forbid—
vulnerable and needy.

But you call me back to reality
where we both know that when I don't
take the time to rest in you, when I
neglect my body's need for rest,
my life spins out-of-control.
Those closest to me could
surely attest to this.

Help me flow with nature's rhythmic dance,
and to trust the darkness as much as I do the light.
Teach me to honor my hunger for solitude,
and quench my thirst to be alone with you.

When I feel overwhelmed, worried, and worn-out,
remind me to let go of the struggle and yield
to my humanity, to my profound need for
divine assistance, and for the rest
that only you can give, the rest
you desire to give
to me.
Amen.

For Reflection, Journaling, or Discussion

1. Children seem to be especially focused on the present moment. Do you think that we adults would be happier—and more spiritually, emotionally, and physically rested—if we were able to live as attentively to the present moment? How would you assess your ability to live in the present moment?

2. Which of the ten suggested ways to prayerfully rest in and with God appeal to you the most? Why? What are some other ways we could rest in and with God?

3. What are some of your favorite memories of playing as a child? How do you play, create, or spend your leisure time now? How would your life be different if you took more time to play and relax?

CHAPTER 7

PRAYING OUR PAIN
AND SUFFERING

*We are patients in the wards of life,
suffering but at the same time
assured of God's . . . care for us.*
—Gabriel Daly, O.S.A.

THE MYSTERY OF PAIN AND SUFFER-
ing is one that we human beings, whether we are
people of faith and prayer or not, wrestle with on
and off throughout our lives. It's an especially
important issue for those of us who are trying to
believe in a benevolent God—a God who is responsive to prayer—because the overwhelming amount
of suffering in the world seems to contradict our
foundational beliefs. Despite countless individual
and communal pleas for help, God sometimes
appears to be uncaring rather than caring, unin-
volved rather than intimately involved, and impo-
tent rather than omnipotent.

Because the mystery of pain and suffering ranks
right up there in importance with the mystery of
God and the mystery of life itself, it has the potential to make or break our faith. As a result of our
wounds, we might turn to prayer with hopes of

obtaining divine assistance, or we may turn away from prayer, discouraged by its seeming inefficacy. The pain and suffering we experience in life might help us recognize our need for God or shatter what's left of our faith as we, out of disgust and disillusionment, give up on God once and for all.

As is true of every other mystery of faith, we are only able to penetrate a very short distance toward the center of the mystery of pain and suffering, just like we are only able to penetrate the earth's crust a relatively short distance. If it were a distance of 1,000 miles to the center of complete understanding into the purpose and meaning of suffering, perhaps we human beings are only able to dig our way to the ten-mile point; the other 990 miles are inaccessible, beyond our ability to comprehend. No matter how much we desire to travel further into this mystery, no matter how hard we hammer away at heaven, at God, and try to figure out why pain and suffering is a part of life, we are stopped abruptly in our tracks. At this point, we need to yield and accept and entrust to God what we cannot know, which, with God's grace, I am only beginning to learn how to do.

The ten miles that we *are* able to travel, however, make all the difference in the world when it comes to our faith and prayer lives. The little bit of understanding we *can* grasp is critical if we are to be people of prayer. Usually our limited understanding of pain and suffering is one we lose and recover over and over. When suffering clutches us in its grip, there seldom seems to be any sense to it, but after the intensity of our pain has subsided somewhat, we sometimes gain some insights and acquire a tiny bit of understanding into what we just endured or survived. Looking back, we frequently recognize signs of God's tender and providential care for us, which were unrecognizable when our pain was most severe. Hindsight not only helps us perceive how God was with us the whole time, it also gives us the deeper vision to recognize the potential gifts that are sometimes left for us in suffering's wake.

In this chapter we will look at how we tend to respond to our pain and suffering and establish some guidelines for wrestling with this formidable foe, who is sometimes a friend in disguise. We will also identify some specific ways to pray our pain so that we might lean more heavily upon God, knowing that we are in the grasp of the one who will always hold us securely. Perhaps we will make some modest headway into the ten-mile zone that is accessible to us, even if it is just one shovelful further into a deeper understanding.

Responding to Pain and Suffering

As unwilling students in the school of suffering, we each cope with life's hurts in our own unique ways. From among the many less-than-healthy choices available to us, we might try to escape or deny the pain, blame our suffering on others, stay busy, isolate, or attempt to numb ourselves with food, alcohol, or drugs. Healthier choices include joining a support group, opening up to concerned friends and family members, dealing directly with our pain, asking for God's help in prayer, or seeking professional help. Sometimes we try a combination of unhealthy and healthy means of dealing with our pain. I some-times make the unhealthy choice of misusing food when I am hurting before I make the healthier choice of turning to God and others for help.

When it comes to our relationship with God, we tend to respond to suffering in one of three ways: we turn away from God, we turn toward God, or we turn away from God for a period of time and then turn back to God.

We turn away from God. Sometimes religious or spiritual people, people of faith and prayer who have been trying to have a good relationship with God, reject God, maybe even for the rest of their lives, because of the depth or breadth or length of their suffering. Those who have lost loved ones to violence, tragedy, or disease are often most tempted to turn away from the God who desires to help them. A single catastrophic event or a combination of significant hurts and losses becomes the straw that breaks the camel's back, snuffing out any flick-ering remnants of belief in a caring, supportive God. While in the midst of our pain we may turn away from God, God does not turn away from us. God knows our wounds and continues to love us, even if we no longer believe in or trust God.

We turn toward God, sometimes for the first time, and allow God to help us. Some of us have drifted away from God or may have never made any efforts or felt any need to have a relationship with God in the first place. When life is flowing smoothly and we have just about everything we could possibly want or need—health, home, family, job, money, possessions—it can be especially difficult to recognize our need for God. But life has a way of dropping us to our knees (needs), abruptly or gradually, as the intensity of our pain becomes unmanageable. Whether we suffer from depression, an addiction or compulsion, alcoholism, an accident, a loss of health, the loss of a loved one, a job loss, a sense of emptiness, loneliness, or a lifetime of regrets, we painfully realize that we can't make it in this world by ourselves. Pain literally drives us to the God who awaits us with wide-open arms.

We turn away from God for a period of time, then turn back toward God. Perhaps some painful or unfair event has caused us to turn away from God. Or maybe well-intentioned yet faulty religious training or unhealed childhood wounds have left us with little recourse but to reject the God of our upbringing. With the passage of time, however, and after the pain has subsided and the anger has been worked through, we are often able to respond to God's gentle tug upon our hearts and turn toward God once again. Although the depth of suffering seems to extinguish all our faith in God, a hidden God-given spark is kept alive within us by God's grace. This tiny spark, like a flashlight on a dark night, can help us find our way back to God. I turned away from God for more than a decade in response to my pain. Pain eventually escorted me back to God, who accepted and embraced me with no questions asked.

Pause, Ponder, or Practice

How do you normally respond to your pain and suffering? Can you recall times when you turned away from God? How about times when you turned toward God?

Coping with Suffering

Imagine a football player who has ninety-five yards to run in order to score a touchdown. He faces eleven huge, fast, hard-hitting opponents who are guaranteed to crush him if he does not receive strong support from his teammates. In a similar manner, suffering can overwhelm and completely crush us if we do not rely on some guidelines for coping with it. Keeping some of the following ideas in mind may be helpful as we pray our pain and suffering.

God does not give us the suffering and pain we experience in life. We are creatures residing in a world in which all living things eventually die. During our journey through life, we human beings inflict much suffering on each other. This suffering comes from us, not from God. Some of our suffering results from impersonal forces such as disease, natural disasters, and accidents. God is not punishing us with the pain we suffer; instead, God desires to be a source of love and support and longs to help us through life's difficult times.

The passage of time is almost always needed when we are dealing with a significant wound. When a doctor sets a broken leg, the passage of time is absolutely necessary in order for full healing to take place. Similarly, prayer invokes the healing power of the divine physician, and time—whether it is a couple weeks, a couple months, a year, or longer—still must pass in order for us to heal. No matter how badly we may want to rush the process, the healing component of time must fulfill its vital role.

When we are hurting, or when we feel sad because of how others are suffering, seeking the support of our friends and family may prove to be very helpful. Suffering is too big of an opponent to face alone. When we allow others to support us, our faith is frequently strengthened, as is our capacity to cope. We need each other to make it through our own pain, including the times when we feel sad for friends or strangers who are suffering.

We need to recognize the signs that point to our need for professional help. I appreciate the support of family and friends, but I don't want them operating on me! Sadness, depression, suicidal thoughts, significant losses, major life transitions, a sense of purposelessness, an addiction, or the death of a lifelong companion often require the help of professional counselors, spiritual guides, or pastors. Through these compassionate and gifted people, God often helps us through our pain. I am grateful for the pastors, spiritual directors, and counselors who have shared their wisdom, compassion, and companionate presence with me during some of my most painful moments.

We can learn how to set our suffering aside for a while when possible. We have some say as to when and for how long we will choose to deal with our pain. Once when I was grieving the end of a relationship, I found it very difficult to attend my college classes. A friend told me to attend class and grieve after class. Or when we are troubled by events in the world, we need to learn how to set our sadness aside after a period of time, so that we don't sink under its growing weight. While we can't turn our pain off and on like a water faucet, perhaps with grace, we can control its flow to some extent, so that we can continue to make a positive contribution to our world. By setting our suffering aside for a period of time—whether it is our own pain or that of someone else—our respite gives us the strength to deal with it again when it is time for us to do so.

We might choose to focus on the aspects of life that are beautiful, uplifting, hopeful, and good. Many people of faith and prayer believe there is much more goodness in people and in our world than there is evil or pain. The media focuses on the world's brokenness, making it easy to be drawn into a skewed, pessimistic view of life. We need to strive for a more complete and balanced picture by setting our sights on the world's wholeness and life's goodness as well. For example, if we find ourselves despairing over the amount of violence in the world, then we need to redirect our attention toward those people, including ourselves, who are making constructive contributions to creation. This doesn't mean we adopt a naive positive attitude and ignore or deny the suffering that is a part of life. Rather, for our own sake and for the sake of others, we don't let ourselves lose sight of the beauty and wonder and hope that permeates life and that God desires for us.

We can learn to set boundaries regarding how much of other people's pain we will allow into our hearts. While we would not want to seal the door to our hearts air-tight, we do need to shut them at times to avoid taking on an inordinate amount of the world's pain. The truth is we can do very little, or nothing, about much of the world's suffering. We need to remember that God is God and we are not. We can feel and extend compassion toward others who are hurting, but we must not take on their pain for it only diminishes our capacity to respond effectively whenever we can. For example, if the pain and suffering we see on the evening news is overwhelming to us, then we might decide to protect our hearts by not watching it or by watching it occasionally. We have our own pain to cope with, and when we take on too much of other people's pain, we are of very little help to them or to ourselves.

When faced with a painful situation, we can discern what is within our power to change and what remains outside our power to influence. This is akin to Reinhold Niebuhr's "Serenity Prayer," which we looked at in chapter 6. While prayer is certainly meant to inspire us to take action on behalf of those who are suffering, we obviously can't help every hurting person or contribute money to every deserving charity or get involved with every worthwhile cause. We have to prayerfully discern where and how we will respond to the needs of some of those who are hurting. And we trust that other good people will also respond as their hearts lead them. As part of the discernment process, we might ask ourselves questions such as: What can I do about this painful situation? What simple actions, if any, can I take? Does this lie inside or outside the realm of my personal power? Is this person, concern, or social justice issue one that seems to be calling me to share some of my time, talent, or treasure?

We can look for and expect to receive some insights into the mystery of pain and suffering from time to time. Perhaps a conversation you have with someone, a sermon you hear, a book you read, or a thought you have will be the key that unlocks the door to a better understanding of what is beyond our complete comprehension. We can and will gain some partial insights into the mystery of pain and suffering if we search for them. God knows all; with God's grace, we can know some.

We can remind ourselves that with God's help, we are strong enough to survive our pain and that it won't last forever. In our most painful moments, we feel weak, vulnerable, and fragile. The end to our suffering seems to be nowhere in sight. At these times, we must allow God to be our strength as we affirm and cling to our inner God-given strength to get through and beyond the pain. Whatever we are suffering, it won't last forever. It will pass as we feel the pain, deal with it, allow time to heal us, and open ourselves to the caring touch of the divine healer.

Pause, Ponder, or Practice
Which of these ten guidelines do you identify with the most? Which affirm what you already believe? Which offer new ideas for you to consider?

Praying Our Pain and Suffering

Before we look at a few ways to pray our pain and suffering, we would do well to remember that prayer does not always—or even usually—result in our pain being taken away completely, although that may be the result sometimes. Prayer is most effective when we combine it with one or more acts of self-care. Prayer often opens us to divine ideas, to our own inner wisdom, so that we might creatively address and cope with our pain. Prayer often reduces the intensity of our suffering and, in some inexplicable way, makes it more manageable. Prayer also helps us regain a sense of God's gentle and compassionate presence when we are hurting.

1. Pray with one of the psalms or in the pattern of the psalmists. The book of Psalms addresses the life situations that are common to people of every era: despair, laments, trust, joy, thanksgiving. Perhaps you will find it comforting to pray with a psalm of trust when you are hurting, Psalm 31 for example, or you might discover a sense of solidarity with the psalmist who addresses God with a complaint or lament, as in Psalm 38. Psalms of lament frequently segue into psalms of trust.

Besides praying with a psalm, we might imitate the psalmists' pattern of praying, which includes both a complaint to God and an expression of confidence and trust in God's saving power. We pour out our pain and suffering to God in great detail, and perhaps after emptying our hearts, we try to express some trust, no matter how weak it may feel to us, in God's power to help us. For example, "Although I have no sense of your presence, loving God, and even though it feels like I am totally alone, I trust that you *are* with me and am confident that you will help me through this difficult time."

2. Pray with Psalm 131. This short psalm, only three verses in length, is an especially good one to pray with when we feel powerless to do anything about the world's pain or helpless to alleviate the suffering of a loved one. The first verse gently reminds us to stop tormenting ourselves by trying to figure out what we can't—why there is so much pain and suffering. The second verse invites us to let God soothe and quiet the intensity of the pain we are feeling for this person or for the whole world, much like a mother comforts her child. The third verse serves as a gentle call to place our hopes in God.

Psalm 131

1 O Lord, my heart is not lifted up, my eyes are not raised too high;
I do not occupy myself with things too great and too marvelous for me.
2 But I have calmed and quieted my soul, like a weaned child with
its mother; my soul is like the weaned child that is with me.
3 O Israel, hope in the Lord from this time on and forevermore.

Pause, Ponder, or Practice
Take a few minutes and prayerfully read Psalm
131 two or three times. If you are presently concerned for someone or feel sad about how people
are suffering in the world, allow God to hold you
and lighten the pain in your heart.

3. Pray with comforting passages from scripture.
The Bible is filled with scripture passages that speak
of God's loving concern for us. As mentioned earlier,
Isaiah 40-55 and the psalms are good places to find
some very comforting verses. We might also pray
with one of the Gospel stories in which Jesus heals a
suffering person. We can place ourselves in the story
and visualize the Spirit of Jesus healing us. You might
want to keep a list of consoling and nurturing verses
handy so that you can easily turn to them in a time of
need.

**4. Name your pain, write it down on a slip of
paper, and place it in your Bible or in your God
box or God can .** We reclaim a portion of the power
pain has drained from us by simply naming and
articulating what we are suffering. "I feel lonely
right now." "I feel hopeless about our world." "I feel

sad about my friend's divorce." Writing it down or composing a short prayer is also an empowering act; its power is amplified tenfold when we engage in some type of physical ritual, which helps us share our pain with God in a symbolic but very real way.

5. Recall how God has helped you in the past, so that you might pray with greater trust in God's power and love to help you through this current moment of difficulty. Because pain is so good (too good!) at getting and sustaining our attention, it forces us to focus on the present moment more attentively than just about anything else. Sometimes we become so caught up in our present-moment suffering, that we fail to remember how God has helped us through difficult times in the past. In short, we forget our own salvation history. Pain can cause us to lose our perspective in life, and weaken our sense of trust in God's caring presence.

But if we fight through the pain of the present moment and recall a time in the past when God helped us, we may find perspective and trust returning to us. We affirm our ability to get through this trying time with God's help, as we say to ourselves, "God was with me during that painful moment, and I was strong enough to survive the pain! God is with me now and I am strong enough to survive this painful moment!"

6. Pray for acceptance, for the grace to surrender and flow with your suffering. Sometimes our suffering is increased when we refuse to accept it, when we resist it, and when we fight it. By loosening our grip on our pain and accepting it as part of life, we may become more receptive to God's healing grace. For example, when we are feeling depressed, it might be much more healing for us to acknowledge our depression and to allow the sad feelings to simply be, rather than to exhaust ourselves by futilely trying to keep these uncomfortable feelings at bay. Although our first response is to resist pain and do everything we can to reduce its magnitude, it is tremendously liberating to reach the point in the process when we can finally surrender our pain into God's hands, knowing that God can heal what we cannot heal in ourselves. And sometimes at the precise moment when we finally let go, God has the room to operate more freely and lead us through the desert of our pain into the promised land of healing.

7. Pray for the grace to recognize the gifts that suffering may have left for you in its wake. Some of our gifts have been discovered as a direct result of how we have suffered in life. We may be more compassionate, tolerant, gentle, forgiving, and wise because of the pain we endured. Sometimes suffering is a friend who practices tough love by waking us up to new possibilities in life. The suffering that is part of losing one's job might become a blessing when we, much to our surprise, discover more satisfying and enjoyable work. The pain that results when a relationship ends might be necessary so that a much more life-giving relationship can unfold in the future. Or when an addiction or compulsion is faced, the intense suffering that is part of the healing process can inspire us to break the chains of bondage and enjoy newfound freedom and joy in life.

There are no magic prayer formulas that will instantly take away our pain. The passage from suffering to joy is a process in which prayer plays a vital, supportive, and complementary role to the caring actions we take on behalf of others and ourselves.

✳ Praying the Chapter

Divine Physician, Compassionate Friend,
The magnitude of suffering in this beautiful,
terrifying world of yours troubles me deeply.

Why so many people have to suffer in such unspeakably
horrible ways tears away at my heart and mind,
shaking my faith to the core. I have hurled a thousand
"why" questions your way, silently screaming and hoping
for an answer, and all I seem to get in reply is
"Return to sender."

I would think that if you want me to
believe in you, you would clue me in as
to what it's all about, but instead my
"why" questions never seem to run out.

Gently free me from demanding to know what I,
and everyone else, cannot know. Help me to accept
my unknowingness while I trust in
your all-knowingness.
Show me how to be a trusting and prayerful

person of faith in the midst of a hurting world.
Restore my vision so that I might also see all that
is hopeful and whole, healing and healthy
in this magnificent world of yours.

Teach me to rely on the support of others
so that suffering doesn't overwhelm and crush me.
Guide me as I discern how I will join my compassion
with yours in responding to the needs of
some of my suffering sisters and brothers.
And, help me to be gentle and compassionate with myself
when I am in pain.
Amen.

For Reflection, Journaling, or Discussion

1. Why do you think God allows pain and suffering to be a part of our world? Have you experienced difficulty letting go of your desire to know what the meaning and purpose of suffering is? Explain.

2. What suffering in our world touches your heart most deeply? How do you pray for or respond to the needs of some of those, near or far, who are suffering?

3. What have been some of your deepest sufferings in life? Are you able to pray or sense God's presence in the midst of your painful times? How has suffering changed you? Have you ever discovered or uncovered any gifts upon its departure?

CHAPTER 8

A WELL-BALANCED
PRAYER LIFE

*Thou that hast given so much to
me, give me one thing more—a
grateful heart ...*
                    —George Herbert

THE MAJORITY OF US ARE PROBABLY
most happy and serene when our lives are somewhat in balance, though what constitutes being in
balance may vary from person to person. Perhaps
in broad terms, we might consider our lives to be
fairly well aligned when we strike a healthy balance between our jobs, our relationships, and our
personal and spiritual growth. When we are in balance, no single aspect of our lives dominates our
time and energy to such an extent that something
else suffers undo neglect because of it. This, of
course, doesn't mean we spend an equal amount
of time in each endeavor, as our jobs—including
the daily commute—tend to require the largest
chunk of time for most of us. Rather, it means that
we are devoting the "right" amount of time and
energy to all arenas of life: working, nurturing our
relationships, fostering personal and spiritual

growth, pursuing our interests, and fulfilling any other responsibilities we may have.

Perhaps the most obvious sign of being in or out of balance is the amount of energy we have. When we are in balance, we tend to have more energy than when we are out of balance. Each of us also has our own unique balance barometers, which indicate how in sync or out of sync we are at that moment in time. One key balance indicator for me is whether or not I am taking some regular time to exercise. Another one is how judgmental I am of others, as that tends to be an offshoot of how I am judging—or not judging—myself. When I am unhappily judging others, it is a clear sign that I am out of balance and a sign of my need to spend some time caring for, rather than judging, myself.

Pause, Ponder, or Practice

What are some of your personal balance barometers? When does your life tend to be most in balance? Most out of balance?

Prayer is one vital component of a well-balanced life. However, the practice of prayer, as with any other endeavor, also has the potential to become out of balance. For many of us, our prayer tends to lack balance when we petition God to such an extent that other important aspects of prayer are unintentionally neglected. And even though the components of a balanced prayer life, as with a balanced life in general, may vary from person to person, perhaps for most of us it includes prayers of petition or supplication, intercession, thanksgiving, and praise or wonder and awe. Our prayer lives also show balance when we allow for some periods of silence, when we pray with the Bible, and when we seek God's forgiveness for the times we fail to love others and ourselves. Another important aspect of healthy prayer is praying with a community of believers, whether we do so in a church setting, in a support group, or with a few friends. Let's take a deeper look at each of these elements of a well-balanced prayer life.

Prayers of petition or supplication. These are prayers in which we ask God for what we need and want. We know that we are not self-sufficient. In fact, we admit to being totally God-dependent. Aware of our need for God's help, we take Jesus' teaching about prayer seriously:

"Ask, and it will be given you; search, and you will find; knock, and the door will be opened to you."
        —Matt. 7:7

We believe that God is our heavenly parent who desires to "give good things to those who ask."
        —Matt. 7:11

God is eager to help us in our daily lives, so we ask with great confidence for what we need this day, "give us this day our daily bread."
        —Matt. 6:11

Prayers of intercession. These are prayers we make on behalf of others. We recognize our interdependence and interconnectedness, and know that other people, like us, are quite fragile and in need of prayerful care. Of course we don't know exactly how our prayers for others are beneficial to them, but we are confident that God hears us and will seek the very best for those for whom we pray. Obviously, we are not informing God of a situation or need that has been overlooked or that has escaped God's attention. Rather, our prayers of petition may simply help us to remember and trust in God's compassionate presence in the lives of others, especially when we are unable to help them in any tangible way. We believe that our prayers *do* have a positive impact in the lives of others, although in ways we can seldom identify or measure. Confident that prayer *does* make a difference, we might choose to pray for some of those we read about in the newspaper or hear about on the news or for the strangers we see on our daily commutes.

One sign of healthy intercessory prayer is that it will inspire and invite us to take loving action on behalf of others. For example, our prayers for a colleague who is going through a difficult time might give us the idea to offer some encouraging words or to send a card expressing our support. Our prayers for the victims of a natural disaster can touch our hearts in such a way that we choose to send a monetary donation to a relief agency who, because of our contribution, can better meet the needs of those who are suffering. Or our prayers for our pastors or priests might compel us to express a simple word of gratitude to them or to speak positively about them when others are speaking critically and negatively.

Also, when we are going through a difficulty, we can be sure that others are going through a similar difficulty, and we might consider praying for them as well as for ourselves. For instance, when we are depressed, we might pray for others who are also suffering the pain of depression. When we are grieving, we might pray for our fellow mourners whose losses are also painful. When we have failed, we offer our prayers in solidarity for others who are in the midst of failure, and so on. A verse from the book of James tells us to "pray for one another, so that you may be healed" (5:16). Our gracious God desires healing for all of us, and Scripture tells us that intercessory prayer helps to heal others as well as ourselves.

Prayers of thanksgiving. These are expressions of gratitude to the one who showers us with abundant gifts and blessings. When we express thanks regularly, our attitude toward life changes for the better. Instead of seeing a world of scarcity in which "I've got to get mine before someone else does," we see the world as a place of abundance, filled with more than enough for everyone.

When we are grateful, the power consumerism has over us decreases, and we appreciate what we do have, rather than lament what we don't have—and probably don't really need. We also tend to complain less often, and we find it increasingly difficult to be around those whose only song is a whine and who thrive on being self-proclaimed victims in life.

When we express thanks to God, our vision improves, and the things we used to take for granted no longer go unnoticed. Among other things, we find ourselves appreciating the great gifts of food, water, shelter, beds to sleep on, and pillows for our heads. Even though we have aches and pains, we tend to appreciate the priceless gift of health and take responsibility for safeguarding it as best we can.

I used to think that gratitude was simply a feeling over which I had no control; it just came and went like other emotions. But now I realize that it is an attitude—a prayerful attitude—toward life. Instead of waiting for the feeling of gratitude to arise within me, I challenged myself to thank God for three blessings each day. The more I did this, the easier it became. Soon I began to see the cup as being half full rather than half empty.

I will give thanks to the Lord with my whole heart; I will tell all of your wonderful deeds.
—Psalm 9:1

Of course, gratitude does not come easy at times. There are incredibly painful situations in life that can seem to snuff out gratitude, and it would be unwise to expect others—or ourselves—to be thankful when caught in pain's excruciating grip. But perhaps our habitual prayers of gratitude will enable us to pass more quickly through the tunnel of suffering or help us to see the cloud's silver lining, which we may have missed in the past.

Pause, Ponder, or Practice

For what are you most grateful? On a scale of one to ten, how would you rate your sense of gratitude? Explain. Consider writing a thank you letter to God for some of the most meaningful gifts and blessings you have received.

Prayers of praise or wonder and awe. These prayers are first cousins to prayers of gratitude. We may feel comfortable exclaiming, "Praise God!" in response to a surprising blessing, or we may prefer to express praise in the quiet of our hearts. As with thanksgiving, wonder and awe tends to be an attitude toward life. We are amazed by God's goodness and by how intimately concerned God is for each one of us. We are in awe of the beauty surrounding us: budding leaves and flowers in the springtime, warm breezes and billowy clouds in the summer, colorful leaves and the crisp air of fall, and the fresh snowfalls and enveloping quiet of winter!

We praise God when we praise a child, compliment a coworker, or affirm our own gifts. We praise God when we show reverence for the earth and do what we can to live more simply and ecologically. We praise God by joining in song with others at church, "Praise God from whom all blessings flow. . . ."

The goodness of our God inspires us to give praise and develop a sense of wonder and awe in life. We don't subscribe to the cultural whine, "I am bored. Entertain me!" Instead, we open our eyes and learn to see again with the wonder-vision of little children, who will stop abruptly, stoop down, and watch the ants scurrying across the sidewalk. We delight in the smiles, the bright eyes, and the heart-melting innocence of these wise little ones.

One summer evening I took my then eighteen-month-old daughter for a walk in her stroller and, upon seeing the full moon looming in the sky, she said, "I want that moon." That was her way of saying, "I want all that life has to offer." It was her way of offering praise to the creator of the moon and the stars. An attitude of praise and wonder and awe is one in which we imitate the wisdom of little children and say yes to God, yes to life, yes to the fullness of life that Jesus says is his purpose for coming:

I came that they may have life, and have it abundantly.
    —John 10:10

Prayers in which we admit our failings and ask for forgiveness. These are also part of a well-balanced prayer life because, no matter how much we desire to take the high road in life, we keep gravitating to the low road. No matter how sincerely we want to do the right thing, we still do the wrong thing from time to time. We want to love those around us but find it difficult, at times, to do so in the circumstances of daily life. We want to be generous and self-giving but end up being selfish and self-preserving; we want to live and let live but continue to judge and condemn others out of habit; we want to speak kindly of others but our craving for gossip overpowers our good intentions.

But Scripture points to the incredibly forgiving nature of our loving God. One story after another, one biblical character after another, one teaching after another, one verse after another proclaims the good news of God's forgiveness for those of us who are sorry for our hurtful words, actions, and failures to act. We can admit our failings to God and confess our sins to God because we know that we are loved in the midst of them. And Jesus says to us:

"Those who are well have no need of a physician, but those who are sick . . . For I have come to call not the righteous but sinners."
   —Matt. 9:12-13

We are all human beings—not perfect beings—who are very much prone to weaknesses. We wrestle with and frequently lose to our persistent character flaws and shortcomings. All of us fall far short of perfection, and any perfectionist tendencies we have can actually become a barrier to seeking God's forgiveness. The tendency some of us have to expect too much from ourselves and to be too hard on ourselves for failing, for not being able to deliver what is undeliverable, makes it unnecessarily hard to accept God's unconditional acceptance—and forgiveness.

We are loved, accepted, forgiven, and embraced unconditionally. No matter how frequently we have stumbled, regardless of how many times we have committed the same sin, or how often we have struggled and failed to break free from a destructive behavior pattern, forgiveness is a gift God desires to give to us again and again and again. Our challenge—and our salvation—is to continue seeking this forgiveness in prayer, confident that our God is not out to judge or condemn us, but to save and befriend us.

Prayers of silence. These prayers are ones in which we can rest quietly in God's goodness. Sometimes we struggle in prayer because we are fumbling around for words when we don't need to have any. How liberating it is for us when we come to this realization: words are not necessary! Of course, many of us have become word-dependent, so we may find ourselves resisting silent prayer initially just like we sometimes resist other new experiences.

I remember how I was in my early twenties and had been resistant to trying Chinese food. Despite many invitations, I refused to try it until a friend almost forced me to. Now, of course, I like it and laugh as I look back upon my initial resistance. Silent prayer, for some of us, may be like what Chinese food once was for me. If so, we can start slowly and gradually and, over time, we will become more comfortable with resting quietly in the silent support of God's love.

As was mentioned in an earlier chapter, using a prayer word such as "Jesus" or "peace" or a prayer phrase such as "peace, be still" or "God, be with me" can befriend us on our journey into silent prayer. Or we might choose to gaze quietly at a picture of Jesus, at a cross, or at a candle to help us become more peaceful and still.

I will admit to not being very faithful to the practice of silent prayer. At times, I find myself searching for words when I have none. I continue to hunger for silent prayer and hope to grow more faithful in my practice of it. The times I have sat quietly in the presence of God, I have felt a hole in my prayer life being filled. Perhaps something in you hungers to sit silently in the presence of God as well. When you and I overcome our initial resistance, we will come to a greater awareness of being loved by divine silence just as we are.

"Be still, and know that I am God!"
    —Psalm 46:10

Praying with the Bible. This is especially helpful when we don't know what to pray, when we don't have anything particular on our minds or in our hearts, so we open God's word to a verse or passage and allow the Spirit to guide us. For instance, we could read and pray with the story of the man born blind in John 9, and listen for how the Spirit might choose to commune with us. We might discover how spiritually blind we are by failing to recognize our own unique gifts—gifts that others see in us. Or we might have our eyes opened so that we "see" someone whom we have disliked in a more compassionate way. Praying with the Bible is also good for most any situation we are facing or any emotional state we are in, whether we are deeply troubled,

worried, guilt-ridden, in need of guidance, longing
for comfort, or filled with joy and gratitude.

*For whatever was written in former days was written for our
instruction, so that by steadfastness and by the encouragement of
the scriptures we might have hope.*
—Rom. 15:4

✓Praying with a community. This is a critical part of
a balanced prayer life. It is a "we" journey we are
on, not an "I" journey. For too many years I never
knew how to spell the simple word "we." I kept
coming up with "I" or "m-e." Perhaps you have
already discovered the value of belonging to a faith
community, but, if you haven't, I hope it won't take
you as long as it has taken me. We are social creatures whose faith and prayer lives are strengthened
when we are with other people of faith and prayer.
It's not always easy to find a community with
whom we feel comfortable praying, but I do know
we must search for it. Among the wisest advice that
has ever been given to me came from a pastor who
told me to "go to the world." Her words continue
to reverberate in me when I revert to sitting back,
hoping that the world will come to me. We need
God and we need a community of others, because
God is often revealed to us in a powerful way
through the unique gifts we share with each other.

*For I am longing to . . . share with you some spiritual gift to
strengthen you—or rather so that we may be mutually encouraged by each other's faith, both yours and mine.*
—Rom. 1:11-12

Pause, Ponder, or Practice

With whom do you feel comfortable talking about spirituality, praying, and sharing your faith? Do you belong to a church or faith or support group? If so, how does it help to strengthen your life of prayer and faith? If you don't belong to a community, what exploratory steps could you take to locate one?

A Final Note

By no means are the aspects of prayer that we have just discussed a complete or exclusive list of what makes up a balanced prayer life. We all have our own preferences—our own unique ways of praying—and we would be wise to heed the oft repeated words of the Benedictine monk, Dom Chapman: "Pray as you can, not as you can't." But perhaps when prayer has become a struggle or a bit dry, we might discern if our prayer lives are missing a vital component that might restore some balance to them and bring some renewed vitality to them at the same time.

We can be assured that the Spirit will be with us and help us renew our prayer lives and draw us ever closer to the one who has called us to be people of faith, hope, love—and prayer.

Praying the chapter

God of Wholeness,
balance seems so elusive.
I am pulled in so many directions
at work, in my relationships, and in
my attempts to care for myself
spiritually, physically, and emotionally.
And so, I tend to lose my balance in
every aspect of my life—
including prayer.

But the good news is
you pass no judgment on me.
Instead, you simply want me to be
whole and well-balanced in
prayer and elsewhere.

Teach me again and again how to pray.
Show me the way to a balanced prayer life,
one in which I thank and praise and
rest with you in prayerful silence.

When I fail and fall for the one-millionth time,
help me overcome my guilt and shame
and ask for your forgiveness once again,
for your unconditional love is oceans deeper
than are my sins and weaknesses.

Finally, loving God,
help me to be a part of a community
of believers and pray-ers, so that we might
strengthen and support each other
on our pilgrimage, on our
journey home
to you.
Amen.

For Reflection, Journaling, or Discussion

1. Of the aspects of a balanced prayer life that we explored in this chapter, which are easiest or most natural for you? Which are more difficult? Which, if any, are missing in your prayer life?

2. What are some other elements of a balanced prayer life that were not mentioned in this chapter? Which of these are important to the way you pray?

3. What are your thoughts or feelings about, or experiences with, silent prayer? Why is it difficult for so many of us? If silent prayer is one of your gifts, consider sharing your experiences with those of us who are more resistant to this type of prayer.

Suggestions for
Further Reading

Walter Brueggemann, *Praying the Psalms* (Winona, Minn.: Saint Mary's Press, 1982).

William Cleary, *Centering Prayers for Personal and Community Prayer* (Mystic, Conn.: Twenty-Third Publications, 1994).

Gary Egeberg, *From Self-Care to Prayer: 31 Refreshing Spiritual Tips* (Mystic, Conn.: Twenty-Third Publications, 1999).

Virginia Ann Froehle, R.S.M. *Loving Yourself More: 101 Meditations for Women* (Notre Dame, Ind.: Ave Maria Press, 1993).

Thelma Hall, R.C., *Too Deep for Words: Rediscovering Lectio Divina* (Mahwah, N.J.: Paulist Press, 1988).

Bill Huebsch, *A New Look at Prayer: Searching for Bliss* (Mystic, Conn.: Twenty-Third Publications, 1991).

Lyn Klug, *All Will Be Well: A Gathering of Healing Prayers* (Minneapolis, Augsburg Books, 1998).

Lyn Klug, *Soul Weavings: A Gathering of Women's Prayers* (Minneapolis, Augsburg Books, 1996).

Carol Luebering, *A Retreat with Job and Julian of Norwich: Trusting That All Shall Be Well* (Cincinnati, Ohio: St. Anthony Messenger Press, 1995).

Bridget Meehan, *The Healing Power of Prayer* (Liguori, Mo.: Liguori Publications, 1988).

Nan C. Merrill, *Psalms for Praying: An Invitation to Wholeness* (New York: Continuum Publishing, 1996).

Chester P. Michael and Marie C. Norrisey, *Prayer and Temperament: Different Prayer Forms for Different Personality Types* (Charlottesville, Va.: Open Door, 1984).

John Powers, *And Grace Will Lead Me Home: A Spiritual Journey* (New York: McCracken Press, 1994).

Ronald Quillo, *The Psalms: Prayers of Many Moods* (Mahwah, N.J.: Paulist Press, 1999).

Joseph F. Schmidt, F.S.C., *Praying Our Experiences* (Winona, Minn.: Saint Mary's Press, 1980).

William H. Shannon, *Seeking the Face of God: An Approach to Christian Prayer and Spirituality* (New York: Crossroad Publishing, 1988).

Carolyn Thomas, S.C.N., *Will the Real God Please Stand Up: Healing Our Dysfunctional Images of God* (Mahwah, N.J.: Paulist Press, 1991).

Jane E. Vennard, *Praying for Friends and Enemies* (Minneapolis: Augsburg Books, 1995).

Sources for Quotations

Page 13: from *New Seeds of Contemplation* by Thomas Merton. New York: New Directions, 1972.

Page 17: from *Clinging: The Experience of Prayer* by Emilie Griffin. New York: McCracken Press, 1983, p. 14.

Page 49: from *A New Look at Prayer: Searching for Bliss* by Bill Huebsch. Mystic, Conn.: Twenty-Third Publications, 1991, p. 3.

Page 62: from *Strength to Love* by Martin Luther King Jr. Minneapolis: Fortress Press, 1981, p. 133.

Page 113: from *Asking the Father: A Study of the Prayer of Petition* by Gabriel Daly. Wilmington, Del.: Michael Glazier, Inc., 1982, p. 96.

Gary Egeberg teaches religion/spirituality in Minneapolis, Minnesota. He is the author of *From Self-Care to Prayer: 31 Refreshing Spiritual Tips* and *My Feelings Are Like Wild Animals! How Do I Tame Them?: A Practical Guide to Help Teens (and Former Teens) Feel and Deal with Painful Emotions*. Egeberg also conducts classes and facilitates workshops, retreats, and seminars in the areas of spirituality, prayer, and emotional health. His e-mail address is: <gary.egeberg2@gte.net>.